TRAVELS IN A DONKEY TRAP

TRAVELS IN
A DONKEY TRAP

by

DAISY BAKER

illustrated by PAMELA MARA

ST. MARTIN'S PRESS
NEW YORK

I T all began with a telegram. "Please phone 01-353 1585. Reverse charges."

We knew this could mean only one thing—our long quest for a donkey and trap might soon be over. What we did not guess was that I, Daisy Baker, seventy-six years of age and living in the remote Devon countryside, was about to make news.

It was the summer of 1970.

The nearest telephone was in the village, two miles away. I could no longer walk that distance so Freda, my daughter, tethered the goats in case they escaped from the field to the garden, as they sometimes do, and set out for the call box, the telegram from the *Daily Express* "Action Line" in her pocket.

We had written to "Action Line" after months of trying to find a donkey to drive. The idea of donkey transport had begun as a sudden brainwave that at first appeared impossible, even laughable, and gradually progressed to the point of possibility, very soon becoming a definite desire.

At first Freda and her husband Eric had suggested a

pony and trap because I was never able to go beyond our acre of garden. Previously I had ridden on the pillion of their scooter, but when unemployment came the scooter was laid up. I soon found that although I had been a good walker in the past the bottom of our lane was now the furthest I could manage.

Even so, I just laughed at the pony idea, but that didn't stop them. Horse sales were discussed, the budget altered to include a magazine on the subject. Ponies became the topic of every conversation.

It was when they were debating the two most important points—whether my few savings would cover the cost, even supposing they could find a pony outfit for sale, and if I could "manage" a pony—that the idea of a donkey came up. A donkey, they decided, would probably be cheaper and also much quieter.

Our knowledge of donkeys was limited to those on the beach. They always walked up and down quietly and obediently, but looked rather small. Could a donkey really pull a cart with someone in it?

"It's how people down here used to travel," Freda insisted, and when Eric said there would be no harm in making inquiries the idea grew. Surely, they said, a farmer somewhere would have an old cart tucked away in his barn, and it should be quite simple to purchase a donkey.

Then it occurred to them that donkeys were supposed to be obstinate. Didn't they have a reputation for refus-

6

ing to move without continual coaxing with a carrot? Unearthing a dusty copy of *Travels With A Donkey*, I was dismayed when I read of the necessity for beatings to get poor Modestine along at a fair pace.

Meanwhile Freda had read a donkey article in a magazine, and had written to ask the writer's opinion of our idea. He put the problem neatly when he wrote back, "As I see it, what you want is a very quiet pony or a very willing donkey." He was inclined to favour the donkey. Donkeys, he said, were not obstinate. They just liked a little encouragement.

The next thing I knew an advertisement had appeared in our local newspaper. It read:

"Pensioner requires donkey and trap, cheap."

It appeared for one week only, and there were no replies. They were quite undaunted. That's all right, they said, this is only the beginning, and began saving up to put an advertisement in a magazine with a national circulation. They telephoned local riding stables, went to donkey derbys, and wrote to a donkey home. Still nothing happened.

Then one day when I was reading the *Daily Express* I suddenly said, "Why don't you write to 'Action Line'? Perhaps they can find us a donkey and trap!"

I had often been impressed by reports in this newspaper column of the varied practical problems that had been solved for readers. Our own letter went next day, and the telegram which had arrived on that summer morning a few days later must obviously be an answer.

After Freda had gone to the village I walked around the garden to think it over, in a state of suppressed excitement. When I reached one of the blue hydrangeas, Betty, the white rabbit who roams free, popped out from beneath it, standing ear-pricked in my path before taking off again with an impudent flip of her up-turned tail.

The sight of her reminded me of all the animals we already had. I reflected, however, that having a large number of animals is rather like having a big family of children—there's always room for another. I tried unsuccessfully to imagine myself driving a donkey. Then I thought of my father. He would have approved of the idea, for in his young days he had been a jockey, and in later years had driven a horse-drawn van for the Anglo-American Oil Company. I was named Daisy after the first horse he rode in a race.

It began to feel as if I had something to live up to, and that driving a donkey as if born to it was what my father would have expected of me. Anyway, I consoled myself, a donkey was hardly likely to behave like a runaway horse I had once seen as a child, the trap it drew knocking down a lamp-post as it galloped past. "Slow and sure like a donkey's gallop"—that would be fast enough for me.

Freda returned from the village, breathless and excited. "They've got you a donkey and a little cart and all the harness—at least, they're in touch with someone who's prepared to let you have it for £75 and deliver it free. It's a marvellous offer. What do you think?"

The suddenness of this quite took the wind out of my sails. I realised that I had to decide whether it was reasonable to part with nearly all my savings in this way, just so that I could drive out in the summer-time. That's if I *could* drive, if the donkey *would* go. I knew the offer was a magnificent one, and I felt grateful, but I thought that, after all, the whole thing was in the nature of an experiment. If I failed in any way, or it didn't work out as we expected, the money would be wasted, and it might be needed for something more important.

It was no use bringing forward all the old arguments—they had demolished these long ago. "You can't drive a donkey on the roads today," I had said.

"You can down here," they'd said. "Why, you'll have it almost to yourself between here and the village."

"There's the cost of food—"

"It's only hay in winter. A donkey can graze with the goats. Just think! You'll have no petrol to buy, no road tax, no driving licence, no insurance!"

"We've nowhere to put a donkey—"

"We're going to turn the shed out. Eric can make a stable door."

Too late for reiterated arguments against the idea, too late to say the money might be needed for something more important. I couldn't have expected a better offer—

I suppose what I had really thought would happen was that the whole thing would have been out of our reach altogether, and the momentary excitement would have gone like a fizz from a drink and I'd have relaxed and said, "Well, there you are. You've tried, and we can't have it, so we'll forget all about it."

Then I thought of my father again. "All right," I said, "let's have it!" And from that moment I had no more doubts.

At that time we had no idea who was letting us have the donkey and cart, and were told that as "the gentleman in question" wanted to be assured that the donkey would have a good home, the *Express* had arranged for the local R.S.P.C.A. inspector to call on us. The shed was cleared with alacrity, and Eric got busy on the stable door. One evening the Inspector called, approved the converted stable, looked at the field and said it was large enough to support five donkeys, beamed, and promised to report that all was in favour of the donkey coming.

The next three weeks passed slowly. I had now completely accepted the fact that I was to have a donkey and trap, and was simply looking forward to meeting the donkey. My donkey! I went back over the years, remembering my father's horses—the pair he worked with on the oil van. Snowball, affectionately known as "Mother", and Prince. Everything came back to me as if I were a child again—his love for them, the attention he gave them, and his anger when Snowball's "honour" was in question.

I had been allowed the joy of a ride with him on one of his rounds, and Snowball was pulling the van alone that day because of the light load. At lunchtime he had stopped at a wayside pub for a pint of beer, and I was left on the high seat, thrilled to be in charge. Several minutes later I was not so sure—Snowball started moving. "Dad!" I shouted. He had already heard the jingle of her bells, and came rushing out. Snowball was halted and I admonished.

"You must have touched the reins!" said my father sternly.

"I didn't!" I protested.

He was so insistent that she wouldn't have moved unless she felt the touch on the reins that I could only suppose I must have moved my hand and touched them accidentally.

Then he calmed down and said, "It was all right, anyway. She would have found her way back to the stable."

I could still hear the pride in his voice, and began to understand a man's relationship with a working animal he is in close contact with daily. Our only "working" animal now was the milking goat, though our little Jack Russell terrier had raised a smile when we bought her and were asked, "Do you want a working dog?" Her mother was an efficient "worker", taking part in the badger hunts that were still organised in that part of

Devon. And now a donkey was coming to "work". Already I began to feel a pride in her, and to anticipate a relationship akin to my father's relationship with his horses.

She was to arrive on the last Monday in September. We had furnished exact instructions on how to find us, for we are tucked away here. On that afternoon the garden was a sun bath, holding the warmth unrippled by cooling winds that so often flow in from the sea. This is the time I like—when, in a good year, even the weather seems to rest, along with the last of the dahlias, the apple trees that have yielded up their fruit, and the harvested wheat fields beyond the pasture land. All summer I had watched the wheat flow with the wind, catching the sun in moving pools of light until it resembled a vast stretch of sand with the tide ebbing.

It is nice here. I watch the seasons change, and was quite contented before I thought of travelling with a donkey. But on that September afternoon when I waited with an almost child-like eagerness for her to arrive, I knew I was looking forward to going to the village to draw my pension instead of having it fetched for me, and that I wanted to go down to the woods again, which I love more than the sea, especially on hot days. I realised what a difference the donkey was going to make to my life.

It was impossible just to sit waiting, so I walked around the garden, under the trees. Someone, long ago, planted them in this acre when it was first claimed from the cattle fields as a garden. A white gate in a stone wall, a white lilac on the right-hand side and on the left periwinkles, teeming in a blue wonderland around a big papyrus plant, banked in stone. That afternoon the tall white candles of the papyrus towered above me, brilliant against the blue of the sky.

Beyond is a small lawn with a horse chestnut tree, and beyond that hydrangea and buddleia. On the right of the gate a path runs to the shed that became the goathouse, with tall fuchsias, red-tasselled, and a rowan tree, red-berried, on the way. Across half the width of the land stride the fir trees. Flowering currant, rhododendron and ferns stand against the wall of the bungalow.

Another path leads up through the little orchard, past a hawthorn hedge, two blue hydrangeas, and the vegetable plot. Near the back, one on each side of the land, are the big sycamores, flourishing in full maturity. Beyond them a little jungle of trees and bushes, and a special corner secluded by conifers.

The steps of the veranda in front of the bungalow (which has its back turned to the gate) lead on to a wide lawn with flower borders, conifers and rowan tree. I went up these two steps and sat down under the little pink roses that ramble in and out of the white trellis, looking out to the great sweep of open sky above the sloping fields. They were green where the bullocks graze, and beyond the hedge stretched the sandy coloured vastness of the cleared wheat field, rising to the sky line. We seem to be held within a circle of sky here, and from the veranda it is possible to run the eye for a full half circle. We are tucked in, as it were, by field and sky, and the effect gives a lovely, safely enclosed feeling.

I looked up the long green hedge that climbs the hill, knowing that presently the top of a van would appear above it, and I should know that the donkey had come.

I began to wonder about her. I wondered how old she was, and where she was born. Didn't donkeys live to a great age? I thought too of her distant ancestry, and I remembered reading that all donkeys carry the mark of a cross on their backs. Perhaps I would call her Martha— Martha, the busy one, the very name for a working donkey and a link with those long-ago days when one of her kind had walked the triumphal way of palms and hosannas.

There was something different about owning a donkey. I was still thinking about it when Freda came and said she was going to write the name of our bungalow on a board and put it at the bottom of the lane as a guide to the van driver.

"Just a minute," I said, and taking the board and the chalk I wrote impulsively in bold letters, WELCOME, DEAR DONKEY. We went down the lane and fixed it up on a tree.

The afternoon wore on and still I kept watch, but it was late when the top of a tall van was briefly visible on the brow of the hill before disappearing between the hedges on the downward slope.

Freda ran down the lane. I followed at what I would now describe as donkey pace, arriving in time to see a friendly-looking young man climbing out of the driving seat.

What had it said in the donkey book we had bought? Something about donkeys being frightened on arrival at their new home, and having to be coaxed out. Something about a battle with a rope.

I waited anxiously.

"Sorry I'm late," said the young man. "There was quite a bit of traffic."

He opened up the back of the van. There was no sign of a donkey. Letting down the tail flap, he went inside, pulling forward a blue and red cart with good rubber tyres and a cushioned seat. Freda helped him out with it while I waited as patiently as I could to see the other part of the outfit.

Going back into the van, the young man opened an inner compartment.

"You can come out now," he said.

As if she understood, a dark chocolate-coloured donkey stepped across the van and down the flap. She was much bigger than I had expected. As she stood by the cart I suddenly remembered she was a trained donkey.

I opened the field gate. The young man gave her a

light slap, and she walked into the field, taking no notice of me at all. Neither did she give her new surroundings so much as a glance. Her nose went straight down to the grass.

"Oh!" I exclaimed. "Isn't she *good*!" And I thought to myself, "I'm sure I can manage her."

We were given a demonstration of how to put her halter on and harness her to the cart. The harnessing looked quite complicated to me. I wondered if I would ever learn to do it.

The young man came up to the bungalow to have some tea, and we plied him with questions. How old was the donkey? Did she have a name? To whom were we indebted?

We had been told a photographer would come too, so there was a pile of sandwiches and home-made cakes —far too many for one young man, but he helped himself bravely under pressure as he answered our questions.

Her name was Darkie, he said, but he didn't know her age. Mr Jim Roberts had sent her from the Donkey Racing Stables in Surrey.

"Would you say," I asked, "that she is young, middle-aged, or old?"

"I would say she's middle-aged," he said.

We talked enthusiastically about donkeys, the racing stables, and donkey derbys, and I counted out the £75. When I expressed my doubts about the harnessing he drew a little diagram on the back of the receipt to help me, and after he had given us Mr Roberts's full address so that we could write and thank him he went off down the lane to the empty van, on his long journey back to Surrey.

When he had gone I took the halter and went to the field to make the acquaintance of Darkie, who was now the centre of the goats' attention. I wondered briefly if I would, after all, change her name to Martha, but decided not to.

I soon found that her behaviour was perfect. That night I led her to the stable, hoping she would approve of her new quarters, and she stepped in as if she had

17

always owned it. The cats viewed her with astonishment, the rabbit with curiosity, the dog with eager interest, but she took everything and everybody quite for granted. I leaned on the lower half of the bright blue stable door and talked to her as she stood looking out into the last of the sunset. Her nose was soft to my hand as I gave her a biscuit, and her large dark eyes looked wise.

Next day her wisdom showed itself in action. I led her to the gate, to go down the lane to the field. At that time we didn't have a gate from garden to field, as we have now. I paused to fasten the latch to keep the rabbit in, and in doing so dropped the rope of Darkie's halter. When I turned round she had started off down the lane at a gallop—a real *horse* gallop, of which she is perfectly capable although she rarely tries. The lane at the bottom carries traffic now and then, so I was in a panic. I thought all sorts of things—that she would run out just as something came along or stray out of sight before I could get there, and that if she wasn't killed or hurt I would lose her. I set off in pursuit.

When I reached the field gate she was standing there, waiting patiently for me to open it. In the one journey up the lane the previous evening she had learned her route, and so it proved to be with all things. She settled down as if she had never known another home in all her long life.

At mid-day the rain came, and with it the photographer, accompanied by a reporter from the local newspaper. The *Daily Express* wanted a photograph of me with the donkey cart. We had just taken Darkie in out of the rain. I got her out again, while Freda brought the cart and the harness.

Plonking the harness down, she looked at me. We both looked at it, then at the donkey and cart, and finally at the photographer. Freda looked at me again, and laughed. "Come on!" she said. "It's your donkey!"

We began sorting out the straps and placing them over the side of the cart, hoping we looked efficient. "Do you remember which is what?" she hissed in my ear. I didn't.

The rain was falling steadily now, so we covered Darkie with a coat, and I went indoors to get my mackintosh hat. I heard Freda hopefully suggesting to the two young men that they come indoors for a cup of tea. They declined, saying they had just had coffee and couldn't stop long.

On my return I found them both standing in a tangle of harness, arguing which piece was which. Between us we experimented with the various straps on the patient Darkie, who stood motionless in the rain except for expressive movements of her tall ears. She probably thought what fumblers we were, but life had evidently taught her that the easiest way with circumstances is to go with them, or, in this case, to stand with them. She was easily the least perturbed of any of us.

I had brought out the diagram on the back of the
receipt, and eventually it was a help. It still seemed to
take a long time to identify everything, but at last the
job was done, and there she stood, wearing all her harness
in what we hoped was the right way, and securely
attached to the cart.

When I climbed in and took the reins the photographer breathed an audible sigh of relief. Freda danced
about waving a carrot to capture Darkie's interest so that
she pointed her ears, the rain fell in torrents, and I
smiled merrily away trying to forget that having been
caught unprepared by photographer and weather alike

I was in my oldest clothes. I consoled myself by remembering that in my day they always used to say that old clothes photographed best.

So there I was, in the newspaper and also on television. The best part of it all was the spate of letters. It had never occurred to me that the story would cause such interest, so I was greatly surprised as well as thrilled to receive a number of friendly letters, an artist's portrait of Darkie, a pound note to buy myself a box of chocolates, and another pound to buy tit-bits for Darkie.

"Your fan mail," Freda called it.

"It's Darkie who's the celebrity," I told her.

When I had answered all the letters I put them away with the rest of my treasures and settled down to being a donkey owner, glad that at seventy-six I suddenly had a new interest.

OUR year—Darkie's and mine—begins on the twenty-seventh of January, provided the weather is fine. To the dark brown donkey it is the day on which she renews her half-forgotten summer activities with the blue cart. To me it is an anniversary.

It is never so cold as it was on that January day in 1894 when I was born. Even the weather welcomed me, my mother would say. All the windows of the house were festooned with icicles.

I smile as I lay out the harness, and rub up the buckles. If I had had my fortune told a few years ago I would never have believed a prediction that in the seventies (mine and the century's) I would be travelling around in a donkey trap.

A birthday should always be celebrated, even when you are seventy-eight, as I was this year. To me no celebration can exceed the joy of that first drive of the year with Darkie. And she is not unwilling. She is contentedly grazing by the hedge lower down the field, one eye at the same time observing me. Her ears are not yet pricked, so she is aware that there is no need at the moment for any sharp reaction to my presence in the field. She will wait for a movement towards her, a sudden call, and then she will stand quite still and upright with her own especial air of donkey dignity, giving me a thrill of pride as if I owned a thoroughbred mare instead of this jenny donkey who pretends, most of the time, to be a humble creature.

Only for a moment will she stand. Then, again denying her humility and misleading me as to her obedience, she will trot away in a semi-circle, head high. But I know that what she is really doing is asserting herself as an individual, independent of me and my demands. The semi-circle leads to the field gate. Once there she stands and waits meekly, all true donkey again. By now we are each well acquainted with the other's little ways.

If we are lucky the sun is shining, and the weather is mild. Often the winter has been wet, and the fields around the bungalow are as green as spring. These are divided by earthed-up walls of stone, green like the fields because they too are grass-clad, or brown with last year's bracken. Later they will be full of ferns and flowers. The wall of the lane leading to the bungalow has hidden within it the seeds of scores of foxgloves, which in July form a procession of flowers from top to bottom. But before that there will be primroses, violets, celandines and red campion.

"Darkie!" I call.

She will come direct only for the biscuit tin, and then

not always. I know there is no need to bribe, so I wait.

She has lifted her head and is regarding me, then lowers her nose to the grass again. As I advance, halter in hand, she stands erect. Her roly-poly body has a line of elegance as she waits motionless, head raised, tall ears on tip-toe with expectancy.

The familiar semi-circle is taken at a quick trot, and she is at the field gate. She stands quite still as I put on the halter. "Good girl!" I tell her, and translate it into donkey language by producing a carrot from my pocket.

When I first harnessed her on my own I was deep in straps for an hour and a half before we started. There seemed to be buckles in odd places, and nothing fitted. I was all mixed up in reins and traces and pondering over what I call the tail-piece and which way the head-gear went.

Now I find it easy, though it still takes a little time. After the lapse of a winter I'm inclined to fumble. She has certainly taught me patience. During the whole of that hour and a half she stood without fidgeting, submissive to my hand as I tried the straps this way and that. Only her ears moved. She seemed to speak with them. Left ear down a bit—what's going on at the back there? Right ear twitching—what *is* going on behind? Both ears bolt upright—it's about time we started . . .

The actual start was a big thrill on that very first outing, the autumn of her arrival. It was not just the fact that I was on the move somewhere after months of garden walks only. The feeling of liberation was more than that. Here was something quite new, releasing in me strange currents of power, as if sitting high in a donkey cart with reins in my hands transformed the mundane me into a totally different person, whose awareness knew wider horizons. It is a thrill that comes again each time I drive out.

Darkie set off at a slow amble. I must admit that beneath the thrill that first time was a slight undermining of confidence—I was, after all, a learner driver! I took confidence mainly from the fact that she was middle-aged, and trained. Imagine, I thought, going out with a skittish youngster, never in harness before. Her leisurely pace exactly suited me.

I was bound for the woods. This was a left turn at the bottom of our lane. Simple. Why panic? First I would rein her in. She was going slowly—it shouldn't be difficult. She would stop instantly, and I would look left and right and then pull slightly on the left rein. It would be as easy as walking round the bend on foot. Then why were my hands shaky, my breakfast-fed stomach quite hollow?

I was painfully aware that everybody on the road would have had driving lessons except me, that the behaviour of their vehicles was predictable whereas the front half of mine had a will and a temperament and secret desires I could only guess at. She might want to stop, eat, turn round, cross over, and it was my responsibility to see that she did none of those things.

Of course there wouldn't be anything coming. It was past the time for the milk lorry and the postman, the butcher's van passed on Thursdays, and the quarry lorries mostly went the other way. There might be a farm tractor, but it would be as slow as we were, and all the holiday visitors had taken their cars home a month ago.

Should I shout "Whoa!"? I tried to remember if my father did. If only I had paid more attention seventy years ago to the way he drove those horses!

I was getting ready to haul on the reins when Darkie herself stopped a few yards from the corner. Her attention had been attracted by another field gate, on the opposite side of the lane to ours. She was viewing this delectable, sheep-dotted pasture with considerable interest.

"Come on, Darkie!" I said, giving the reins a gentle shake. It was a pity to have to start her up and stop her again almost immediately, but there was nothing else for it. I couldn't see along the road at the bottom.

Darkie moved slightly nearer to the left, towards the gate. "No!" I cried, shaking the reins. "This way!"

She stopped.

I wondered if I might allow myself to climb out and lead her round the corner. But no. It had to be done properly.

"Darkie," I coaxed, "come on." She shook her ears,

removed her fascinated gaze from the field, and walked on. The next moment I was pulling on the reins shouting, "Stop!" Obligingly she did so.

We waited, and I looked both ways and listened. It seemed necessary to listen in case anything was coming in the distance, as I didn't know how long she would be turning left, or even, for that matter, if I could get her to turn left at all.

I kept telling myself it was simple, and of course it was. All I did was pull the left rein a little, say "Come on, Darkie!", and we were round the corner. The next minute there we were, if not exactly bowling along, making steady progress in a straight line on the left-hand side of the lane. I relaxed, and reflected that this must be a lot easier than driving a car.

And then she stopped. Although I had thought of this happening I had forgotten it when we headed so nicely for the woods, and I was taken by surprise. But what did it matter? There was no impatient queue of cars behind so she could stop if she wanted to, provided she obliged me by starting again. She certainly had plenty of temptation. The grass along the bank was thick and green and long, and her nose was busy searching out the richest blades. I let her munch a mouthful, then gave the reins a reminder flip. We were, after all, on a journey. She took another mouthful, shook her ears, and walked on.

In this fashion we went our way. When the green bank gave way to a dense wall of hedge bordering the beginnings of the wood there were no more stops. I was all contentment, filled with the peace that filled the lane and glad that our progress was at a pace to allow me to prolong this pleasantness. Yes, I decided, it was far more agreeable than rushing through in a closed car.

I was lucky in being one of those for whom the speed of a journey was its least important aspect—I didn't have appointments to keep and I was under no pressure from time in any way, for it wouldn't really matter if I were late home to dinner. I felt I had slipped back a century, or at least to the days of my childhood, when the pace of life was so much more relaxed. For here I was, moving through the lane at a lingering pace, needing neither to brake nor accelerate, feeling as much a part of it all as the rooted trees and the magpie flashing black and white just beyond the donkey's nose.

This feeling of being a part, of belonging, as it were, in the universe, was one to cherish and if possible expand, for it gave a sense of safety and a kind of knowing that underneath the surface of things all is well. I was not rushing through shaking the dust off my feet, for every yard of my journey had as much importance as my arrival at the end of it. The woods would come, or I would come to the woods, with a thrill of satisfaction and fulfilment. None of this would have occurred to me had I been whisked there by car. I had a sudden great affection for Darkie, and would have liked to stroke her nose there and then. She, as apparently unconscious of me as I had been of her for a moment, dreamed along to her unknown destination.

My meditating was interrupted by an unexpected purring of sound right out of context with the atmosphere I—or the donkey—had evoked. I must have looked rather disbelievingly at the car that appeared suddenly round the next bend in the lane. But there it was, solid enough, and as it approached I realised there was not room to pass. I'm not sure if Darkie stopped first or if I stopped her. She, at any rate, was less perturbed than I was, behaving as if she encountered cars every day of her life. I was the one who looked as if I'd never seen one before.

To the car driver I must have been even more of a surprise. Smiling broadly, he started to back. I had to make the next delicate manoeuvre—that of getting Darkie to start at the right moment, and as he signalled me on I prayed she would obey me. When she did not I nearly panicked and got out to lead her, but with a bit more encouragement she was on her way and the car driver and I were saluting each other like old hands on the road.

And so we made the woods. It is the shortest and easiest of our journeys, and it is there that we go on our first trip of the year at the end of January. For both of us it is a favourite way. In winter we appreciate the depth of the lane cut between the high banks and so affording us protection from the fresh winds that sweep the fields, and when the wind changes and the misty drifting rain draws curtains over the landscape we huddle along the tunnelled lane in comparative comfort. Then there are those January days of unexpected enchantment when the sky is summer blue for an hour or two, and at home the sun is so warm in the shelter of the veranda that I eat my meal there.

Down to the bare woods in this soft air I always half expect to see leaf buds breaking into green. But not yet. There will be many days of contrary weather before the morning trip to see the first hint of new leaves in the woods. Meanwhile I enjoy the beauty of the branches themselves, loving their outline against the sky, the intricate tracery of twigs invisible later in the year when they are leaf-clad. In and out of the pattern of the boughs go the bluetits, easy to see now however high they flit. Their head feathers seem to rise slightly in surprise as they turn a bright eye down to me, for a person in these woods is rare, and in winter unknown.

I always leave Darkie tied by the gate of the field that leads down to the wood. On that January trip I gave her a mound of hay, and she munched slowly and contentedly. Even so she lifted her head to observe the direction I took.

At the bottom of the field a little wooden bridge spans a stream. I paused to lean on the rail and look down on the water, brimming to its banks and tumbling over stones in a miniature waterfall. And I suddenly found myself marvelling at the *life* in the stream and thinking how much throughout the years I had taken merely for granted.

I wished then to see everything as if it were for the first time. Yet I meant more than looking with the wondering eyes of a young child. Now it seemed there was another way of seeing—with awareness of the identity of everything linking at the same time into a whole, of which I too was a part.

I looked at the aliveness of the water, and it was new to me. There were words struggling deep in my mind so that I wanted to dig them out of that recess of unconsciousness and bring them to the light of conscious thought. I was vaguely aware there was a connection with the donkey. There was an importance about the donkey that I could not quite place. I watched the sun rays shiver on the water as I pondered. They seemed to laugh with brightness as they shivered, and the words came up from the water, or from the even greater deeps of my mind. "The stones would cry out", were the words. I remembered there was a donkey-ride in triumphal procession, and I marvelled on the life that is in the stones too—the stones on that road of long ago and the stones under my feet.

Presently I left the stream to the sunshine and entered the wood through the wicket gate, thinking over all this as I followed the path that leads to the tallest trees. Here I was dwarfed, but my inner stature was high, reaching

31

up the height of the trees themselves. I smiled, remembering a high staircase when I was a child, and how I would
sit on the third step up, enclosed by the narrow staircase
walls, the door at the bottom closed and the bedroom
doors closed on the landing at the top.

Secure in being alone for a while I would gaze up at
the lofty ceiling, my head thrown back until my neck
ached, thinking about eternity, which I had heard about
at Sunday school. Eternity that had no beginning and no
end, but went on for ever and ever . . . the high staircase intensified my impression of it as I stared upwards
until I felt dizzy, and went back to play with my dolls—
Roy Burton, the teddy in short trousers, Rosie Dale, the
big doll with the pink china cheeks, Mavis Pettitt, of the
flaxen hair, and many more I could no longer remember.
They all had surnames because they went to the

"school" at which I was the teacher, and I compiled a register and sat them in rows on the sofa.

There was Dobbin too—the little wooden horse who had belonged to those far-away days of childhood which seemed little more than a dream. And now I was getting old and had a donkey instead of a wooden horse, and I knew that these days too would become a dream—and after *this* dream would I actually awake into an unchanging reality that would never depart from me as these phases of living were passing?

I could ask my questions of the trees all day, and tomorrow find more, and the trees would not answer, but would instead give me their deep sense of peace and of strength, more satisfying even than answers. Particularly the leaning tree—that vast trunk growing at so strange an angle and yet succeeding at its topmost point in penetrating its neighbour's growth to reach skywards, those top branches as free in the air and light above the wood as the tall straight trees that had grown direct towards the sky.

The strand of sunlight threading through bare boughs had already moved from where I stood, and I was reminded that I needed to be out on the road again if I wanted to be home before the brief warmth had gone out of the day. As I turned a grey squirrel fled before me down the path of leaves, vanishing up the grey trunk of a beech, into which he appeared to merge.

My thoughts adjusted to the ordinary level of matter-of-fact things, just as in those dream days of childhood I had turned from my awestruck contemplation of eternity on the staircase to a game with dolls. I crossed the little bridge over the stream without lingering, and there at the gate stood Darkie, patiently waiting with the cart, which Eric had painted all blue, also making a little door in the side so that getting in and out was easier. Darkie was no longer eating. Her ears were up, and she was obviously expecting me. As I called she turned her head to greet me. She was as willing to make for home as I was, and we set off at a steady pace, which she kept up all the way, for she seldom pauses on the homeward journey.

Unharnessed, she followed me into her stable for hay. I could smell curry as I passed the kitchen door, but it would have to wait. The garden bluetits were flying around me as I went down the path, and the calling of the chaffinches rang insistently. These birds recognise me, and as they expect a plate of food to appear every time I do this would have to be my next job after putting the harness away.

As I prepared the crumbs and fat to throw on the high, flat roof of a shed away from the cats, I remembered another garden even more filled with birds than this one. And that had been a town garden. Bluetits and greenfinches had come then. It had started with two ounces of peanuts, and it ended with nine pounds a week at the height of the winter.

Freda and I were living alone then, in a terrace house fronted and backed by more terrace houses. We had a little garden between privet hedges, and seeing a single bluetit one winter day we hung a dozen shelled peanuts strung on cotton from the clothes line.

Two tits came, then four. Soon a dozen were chasing each other to and fro off the line, swinging on the nuts two at a time, with a third at the top, pecking downwards. We increased the supply. Gradually the greenfinches came—just a few at first, and then suddenly in dozens, scores, and eventually fifties. All day long there were relays of birds assembling on the roof-tops and filling the two clothes lines now closely hung with nuts. The greenfinches could not swing on the nuts as the bluetits did, but they learned to sit on the line and reach down to eat, and even to hook up a whole string of nuts under one claw. We always hung the nuts instead of strewing them on ground or table because it was a cat-haunted neighbourhood. The long lines filled with birds was a thrilling sight.

There was continual activity as they came and went throughout the daylight hours, occasional squabbles and constant changing of places, queues on the opposite roofs awaiting their opportunity, and always another bird to take a vacated string of nuts. I spent hours threading them.

Peanuts were eightpence a quarter in the old currency at that time, and the birds were costing twenty-four

35

shillings a week to feed. We thought it worth it, even when Freda's job threatened to finish.

"If I had any sense I'd save that twenty-four shillings," she said one day. "Sounds mad, spending it all on peanuts every week. But I can't do it, Mummy— I can't let them down in this weather. Things will work out somehow."

We had always said that—things will work out. And they always had. Now here we were in this beautiful Devon countryside, in a new home and a new life, with our family of animals. Much had come out of emptiness. I was glad we had gone on spending that money on peanuts. We had never missed it, and although still managing on little money the key word was *managing*.

I had all I wanted—even a donkey and trap.

AS the days grow longer so do my travels. But the distance is greater only by a mile or two, for unlike those of Stevenson's reluctant donkey, Darkie's journeys are confined to the immediate neighbourhood.

The woods are barely half a mile away, the village two. A four-mile trip to a beach, making eight with the return journey, is the furthest she has been.

At the start of her village journey she has a hill. Like Modestine, her pace then is "something as much slower than a walk as a walk is slower than a run", but unlike that famous donkey driver, who went on foot, I don't suffer as he did—"it kept me hanging on each foot for an incredible length of time; in five minutes it exhausted the spirit and set up a fever in all the muscles of the leg." I am high on my cushioned seat, and being in no hurry have no occasion to fret.

I have never tried shouting "Proot!", which Stevenson describes as "the true cry or masonic word of donkey drivers", nor do I pluck a switch from the hedge and "lace her about the stern-works". She goes up the hill at

her own pace, stops when she feels like it, and has a
snack from the hedge now and then, and if I feel she is
taking too much advantage of the situation I jerk the
reins a little and talk to her a lot in encouraging tones.
Thus we arrive at the top of the hill, and here we wait

for a few minutes' rest for her while I have the pleasure
of looking back at the landscape, following the skyline
as far as the eye can see.

Now we travel a level road, and when we reach the
spinney I look out for the owl who observes me sometimes from a branch he believes to be out of reach of my
view. I do not look directly at him—a kind of sideways
look, artfully encouraging Darkie at the same time to

browse just there, and we being such a placid pair he remains undisturbed. Perhaps it is the donkey he is eyeing with such a concentrated stare.

A car behind us, and there is a gap where the owl's face was, and as the car inches by a smiling face is looking up at me and someone is quite likely to say, "How nice—a donkey!" Often a car will stop alongside the donkey cart, and I find myself conversing with the driver and passengers as if we are old friends. The warmth of feeling in the common interest of the donkey does me good.

We reach the downward hill, which helps to quicken her pace, and I look out for the hedge gap which frames a green and blue picture—a glimpse of the fields beyond the hedge climbing skywards to the east and to the west gently sloping down to cradle the sea. This road carries more traffic than the lane, especially in summer, but it is much wider until it narrows towards the bottom, and we all travel in comfort without the slowness of the donkey cart obstructing the fast vehicles.

Darkie does not mind them. She looks neither left nor right, ignoring the cars completely and no longer seeking to eat from the hedge. Her head is set for the village, and she keeps up her steady pace. I feel wonderful, sitting back holding the reins. Once a coach tour of elderly people came up the hill as we were going down—two coaches, and at every window faces that lit suddenly with joyous smiles at the sight of me out driving with a donkey. Hands waved, the driver slowed, someone stood up with a camera, and the coaches were filled with laughing voices. A memory this for the dull days—for them too, I wonder?

The road winds round to the village, past a stream almost hidden under canopies of rich green grass. It was this grass that lured Darkie one day on the way home so that she nearly tipped me into the stream as she reached for it and brought our left wheel to the edge of the bank. It was no skill on my part or good sense on hers that saved us from this mishap—just luck. As she went on again the wheel slid down on to the road, having missed the extreme edge by no more than the width of a grass blade.

I found myself recalling a holiday outing from those distant childhood days. My uncle and aunt had hired a pony trap for the afternoon, and in it we all piled joyfully—my father and mother, my brother Victor, and me. Uncle Arthur was driving, and we went at a brisk trot along the dusty country lanes in the hot August sunshine. "Let me drive!" cried my little Aunt Clara, who even in those days could well have been a forerunner of Women's Lib. She took the reins, her bobbed head held high, and urged the pony to his best efforts—and before we knew where we were the trap had slid off the road and we were all in the ditch.

Strange how the years roll away as the donkey cart rolls along. Darkie links me continuously with the old days. And so with all the interest of the journey, the friendly greetings on the way, and the memories, it seems no time at all before we are passing the village church, and I am glancing up at the clock—as if time mattered! All that matters is if the shops are still open and even then if their owners have gone to lunch we can wait, Darkie and I, driving around the village to look at the cottage gardens.

I leave her by the churchyard wall while I collect my pension, and she contentedly rubs her neck against one of the shafts of the cart. She is quite ready to turn round when I come out again, and shows signs of eagerness to start along the homeward way. By the Vicarage wall she pauses, her eye on the shop across the road. She knows that her friend Mrs Steele, will come out and cross the road to her with a handful of carrots. Darkie's gentle lips close over the one she is offered and her big teeth crunch slowly. As soon as one has gone her nose is extended for another . . . and another . . . and another. Eventually, after carrots and conversation, we leave the village behind us.

If it is summer we are much longer than our two main stops. There will be children around the village, and holiday visitors, and Darkie is the centre of interest. I submit half a dozen times to having our photographs taken. Few people say "May I?"—just level a camera at us, and though this was embarrassing at first I smile to myself as I think that nobody says "May I?" to a celebrity either, so I'm obviously receiving film star treatment. Darkie and I are part of the scenery of their holiday—let them photograph us as a sight they will probably not see again, and go away happy in having secured an unusual picture. I've even given up hoping my hat's straight. I just hope that at the crucial moment Darkie's ears were erect. A donkey with her lovely furry ears on tip-toe with alert interest is worth a photograph.

"Is she yours?" the children ask. "May I stroke her?"

"What's her name?"

"Why do you ride in a donkey cart?"

And one woman asked, purse in hand, "What are you collecting for?"

The cars move on, the church clock strikes, the children run off or are led reluctantly away. Darkie and I move slowly on towards the hill. She will go up, then down, and so home to her field where the first thing she does when her harness is off is to go to her favourite bare patch of earth and roll on her back, legs waving.

That bare patch in the field, now four foot square, began as a mole hill. Susy, the terrier, dug in it, sniffing furiously, and when she came away with earth on her nose the cats walked on it, and sat round in patient vigilance until King Billy, head of the goat family, came along. Left hoof raised—he always uses this one, so are goats left-footed?—he proceeded methodically to smooth the earth before sitting on it. Since then all the goats and Darkie have worked away on that patch of earth, scraping at the grass until they eventually achieved this sitting and rolling place.

Does Darkie dream of that moment when she will roll, free of her harness, as she plods up the hill? She never attempts to hurry, though on the other hand she seldom pauses, as on the outward journey, for snacks from the hedge. Little pauses for a rest, and then on again until we come level with the hedge gap that reveals the sea, and we are nearly at the top. Once she galloped about here.

We were not quite at the gap, and she had paused, when a thunderous sound came from the other side of the hedge, and she, unmoved by lorries changing gear and motor cycles roaring past, suddenly lifted her head, picked up her hooves, and galloped, heedless of hill or cart, not slowing until she had passed the gap.

It is always the unknown that frightens. If she could have seen through the hedge she would have remained unmoved. On the other side of it were bullocks, and they had suddenly come crashing down against it. She is unafraid of other animals, and is well acquainted with bullocks as they are her next door neighbours at home.

How pleasant it is on a spring afternoon to turn into the narrow lane beneath the beech trees. The spring is late coming to the hedge, but even when this is still brown and apparently dormant the high banks beneath its roots have thick new grass blades of the deepest green among the winter-bleached growth of last year, and here and there the sunlight falls on little light green cushions of moss. I muse on the life that teems within just a yard of bank, so the whole of it, from the top of the hill to home, must be quite a universe.

Here, in summer, I will see a tiny lizard sunbathing. There must be many scores—even hundreds?—of inhabitants invisible to those of us who pass by, even at donkey pace. There are the insects—I catch glimpses of leggy spiders high-stepping it over leaves or mountaineering on a grass blade. There are the little creeping ones like the scuttling wood lice which, as children, we always called cheesey-bugs, and which amused us by rolling into a ball when touched with an inquisitive finger. Then there are the field mice and the delightful little pig-nosed shrews that can nip a finger. I know these inhabit the bank, and I know they nip fingers, because I rescue them sometimes from the cats. They are not easy to save, for they give up quicker than a mouse. I once pursued a cat with a field mouse for half an hour, and the mouse lived to run away. There is a trick worth knowing if an attempt is to be made to save a victim, and this is especially useful in spring when fledgelings are so easily caught.

At first the captured one is lightly held in the cat's mouth, for the cat's idea is to preserve its life for the pleasure of play—to drop it and pounce and pick it up again, for as long as possible. I strongly resist the desire to grab the cat, for I know that pressure on its own body will cause it to bite hard on the small creature I am trying to save. So I adopt the cat's own tactics. I stalk and watch my opportunity and—pounce! One hand firmly over the cat's face, the other under its chin. Like this the mouth can be forced open. It can be easy and it can be difficult. Much depends on the cat's awareness of the intention, and so on its evading tactics and final resisting power, which can involve a front paws' battle, the fighting claws trying to encircle the released captive as it falls from the opened mouth.

Only one of our six cats fights like this. Of the six only three are hunters, and of the three only two live to hunt. Once "pounced on" the two will submit to my greater power, and I have the pleasure of seeing a bird actually fly straight out of their mouth, or a mouse jump out and run away.

The hunting cats know the life that teems in the banks. They stroll slowly up the lane and down, sharp-eared, keen-nosed and alert of eye. A slight rustle will stiffen them into poised expectancy, a scent captures their whole quivering attention, and the barest perceptible movement of the grass will provoke an investigating paw thrust deeply in.

Always they bring their trophies home—sometimes staggering in with a black-coated, pale-handed mole, or even a young rabbit. Once dead, their interest has gone. They seldom eat what they catch, but the young kitten is intrigued by the catches and I am saddened when I cannot save. Yet I know there is truly no need for this.

How little do we really comprehend of life. I do not love the mole—it is the life within the mole, expressing itself as mole, that I love. The life withdraws from the harmed body, but still must be life, for the body responded only to the inhabiting power, now gone. Gone where? The life power itself cannot die. So I bury the mole in leaves and grass and think a benediction for it, believing it moves with greater freedom in some eternal place, or will in time again know the earth it has left in the same body form, or perhaps another. For life must live.

I think of all this as we go down the hill, and I look from the furthest horizon to this universe in miniature—the bank below the hedge. How little do we know of the lives of its inhabitants—and they know nothing of ours! I ponder on the fact that there is so much more to living than we can possibly comprehend. Meanwhile here is my wise donkey, concerning herself only with the need to journey on so that she may return to her field and stable.

COMES a day in summer when the sky is blue all over, and the pink fingers of the unopened honeysuckle down the lane promise soon to release the hidden scent. On one such day I walked in the warm air and noticed that only a soft wind was breathing through the fir trees after the many leaf-streaming, draughty winds of spring that always manage to steal down the collar of my coat and around my ears. The landscape basked in the sunshine, and I knew that this was a day for the sea.

The animals were happy. Susy was expectantly at my heels, the cats had made nests for themselves in long grass. I saw the tips of the white rabbit's ears as she burrowed in the rockery. Beyond the field fence two of the goat family were in their sitting place, King Billy standing down the field near Darkie, who was grazing with waving tail to fan away the flies. He often leaves the goats to stand near her, apparently taking great pride in being seen in her company. Darkie tolerates his presence but never encourages it. Against her dark chocolate brown he is a handsome figure in his light brown coat, his silky beard turning to gold as the sun catches it, his short, upright tail golden, his curving horns sun-tipped with silver.

Regal he may look, yet I know his behaviour will be roguish. He has to be tied before Darkie is called and the cart taken into the field, and so does the nanny and her kid. All are inquisitive, standing on hind legs to inspect the cart and even trying to climb into it.

It was a day for cars. As it was the first summer trip I felt pleased and excited at the prospect of a busy road, a crowded beach, after the quiet, empty lanes. For the moment I had done my dreaming on our solitary outings —the time had come to meet the world again, to see plenty of people, to share enjoyment. Just as later I would seek with relief the stillness of the woods on a hot day when the teeming road and the bright beach had lost their allure, so then I set out to look upon the other face of summer. The winter and the slow spring had been long, and I felt as joyous as a child on a special treat.

Darkie stepped out willingly. Perhaps she knew she too had treats ahead, for the banks were lush with growth and her hedge snacks would be deliciously varied—the special broad-bladed grass that she likes, beech leaves and oak, bramble and campion. And in the cart I had her bag of biscuits and carrots. On the way I would gather an armful of long grass and hedge pieces to occupy her for the half-hour or so spent on the beach.

I took sandwiches and a raincoat—*that* wouldn't be needed, but I like to take it—and felt all set for the day. We could be as long as we liked. Or as long as Darkie liked. I revelled in the absence of time in my life. It would be hours before dark, and the closing of the day is the only aspect of time I need to heed.

I wore my watch, but more because I am used to doing so than to check our progress. That watch is as much part of me—actually more so—than my coat. I have had it for nearly sixty years. In the First World War I knew two brothers, Fred and Bill. Fred was a soldier, Bill a sailor. "Ah," said their father, when I walked out with Fred, "all the nice girls love a sailor. You wait till Bill comes home. You won't want Fred then!"

"Yes, I shall!" I declared indignantly.

Fred was still only seventeen when he enlisted in 1914, putting his age on in the patriotic fervour of the boys of that generation who could not wait to volunteer to "fight for their country". We planned to marry after the war.

Before he went away he suggested buying me a special present, and asked which I would like—a watch or a new bicycle. We cycled a good deal in those days, sometimes going down to Dorking from London, but even so a new bicycle didn't tempt me. I chose a watch because it would be something to keep.

Past the flower and fruit stalls in Walham Green we went one Saturday. It was no uncommon sight in those days, a young soldier with a girl on his arm shyly entering a jeweller's shop, and the elderly man behind the counter greeted us benignly. Fred asked for a gold wrist watch.

We were shown two watches, one plain, the other with red stones set round the face. The jewelled one was £12 10. o., the plain one £10. I knew at once which I wanted. The plain one was smaller, and I liked it and thought it would be more serviceable than the one with stones.

"Are you sure?" asked Fred, picking up the jewelled one. "Wouldn't you like this one? You can have which you like."

He thought I was thinking of the price, but I said no, I really did like the plain one best. So we bought it, and the shop-keeper, putting it in the self-same case in which it rests today when I'm not wearing it, remarked smiling, "You've made a good choice. You couldn't wish for a better little watch to wear on your wrist."

In 1917 I was glad I had chosen a watch instead of a bicycle. Although it was so small a comfort when the news of Fred's death came, at least I had a real keepsake of the precious years of his life.

After that I was doing daily domestic work at a house in Chelsea for a pleasant middle-aged woman who always shared the work with me. One day she remarked, "Are you going to be like the Queen, Daisy, and marry his brother?"

And so it turned out to be, for in 1921 I married Bill. Fred had said in a letter to Bill, "Look after Daisy for me." And he did, for seventeen years, until the beginning of the illness that eventually parted us.

On that summer morning I suddenly thought of Fred's bicycle that I might have had. Even if I had it still, which was most unlikely, I certainly wouldn't have been able to ride it down to the sea. But I had the watch on my wrist as I went down in the donkey cart, and the jeweller's words were right. It is as good now as it was then.

I thought of how Bill had run away to sea when his father married for the second time. He was in the Navy before the 1914 war broke out, and after the war he had another eight years' service to do. Although we married in 1921 it was 1926 before he left the Navy.

He was lucky in getting a job straight away, becoming a porter at a London club. We were then living in Chelsea, in a block of buildings, since demolished, known as Onslow Dwellings. Bred in the country, I often longed to live there again, and felt grateful that we had our flat on the top balcony—a corner site, too. I made a little garden in a window box.

The country dream persisted, but when Bill put his name down in the hope of becoming a London postman it looked as if it would remain a dream. Life was restricted in that top flat. Bill went to night classes and learned carpentry, but there was nowhere at home to make things. The slightest noise would disturb the neighbours. I could at least get my little bit of country in the London parks, where I pushed the pram every day, but Bill, despite his love of reading, disliked the inactivity the flat imposed upon him.

And so we decided to buy a house in the country. I had made efforts to do so before, and this time we were successful. In 1931 we moved fifteen miles out of London to a quiet country lane among fields and woods. We were buying the semi-detached house on a mortgage. It was a new house, having been built six months previously. We put down a deposit of £100 and it was ours. The price was £450.

We were situated about a mile and a half from a village and the railway station. Bill continued his job for a time, walking over the fields in the early morning to catch the "workmen's train" to London. When he was home he now had plenty to do in making a garden. A long stretch of what had been woodland went with the house. The builders had cut down most of the trees and left the stumps. Bill, armed with pickaxe, had first to dig up all the tree roots before he could even think about cultivation. Eventually he achieved a beautiful garden, back and front, and with innumerable old-fashioned roses blooming in the summer the house lived up to the name we had chosen—Rosegate.

Bill gave up his London job after a time and worked locally. He had a succession of local jobs, one of the first being on a farm. This was hard, both in winter and summer, possibly more so for a man not bred to it. In winter there were many mornings of handling frozen vegetables, and in the summer he toiled long hours in the heat. That summer, as he had been ill, I used to take his dinner down to him in the fields instead of giving him sandwiches. This necessitated a cycle ride of about six miles there and back.

I would have the main course in an aluminium basin —how vividly I recalled those times the other day when I realised that the self-same basin is still in use after over thirty years. When Bill left the farm I made the Christmas puddings in it. Today it serves as a goat bowl.

Bill would be so tired that when he had eaten his meal he would lie flat on the grass and fall asleep in the hot sun. Summers always seemed to be hot in those days. When the short dinner hour was over I had to wake him and tell him it was time to go back to work.

He left the farm to work at the railway station. I was interested when he came home and said he took out a horse and cart to deliver parcels, little guessing that one day I would drive out in a donkey cart. I don't think either of us would have believed that then. Bill dreamed of the day when Freda might own a little car and run us to the seaside, but it was not to be. He had a spell in hospital, and then worked as a groundsman at a school until he died.

The memories come and go, but when we left our lane, Darkie and I, on that first summer trip the past vanished as if a curtain had been lifted on to a new scene, for here we were on a road filled with cars, all going to the sea. At once we became involved with the constant noise, the faces at the windows, the waving hands of children.

I really felt we had come right out of the past—my past and Darkie's too. Their packed cars, overflowing with children and luggage, with here and there the gay paraphernalia of tent equipment or a vividly painted boat on top, the sound of their engines and the smell of petrol brought me right back into the present-day world, of which Darkie and I, for all our apparent other-worldliness, are a part. Yet even as this flowing stream of vehicles caused the transformation for me, my gently plodding donkey cart had the reverse effect for those who flashed by, transporting them backwards in time, to their obvious delight. They would appear to have all the advantages, for they would reach the sea long before I did, and most of them had money to spend. But they were thrilled to see this age-old method of travelling, and I have found, during the course of my journeys, that most people I speak to tend to say the same thing—how lucky I am to have a donkey cart, how they wish they had one, how much better it is than a car.

I tell them that it's all right if one has plenty of time, but no use for keeping appointments. And they reply gaily that time is of no importance, and just to go and get there is enough, and they would not mind changing their cars for what they indicate is a superior form of transport.

I smile and nod and indulge them, and do not remind them about their city jobs and all the other people's cars and the awkwardness of parking, and the busy tenor of their full lives compared with the quiet routine of mine, for I know that this donkey transport dream is similar to the old cottage-in-the-country one with which many town dwellers have coloured the street-encompassed hours of monotonous routine. In dreams there is only colour in the picture, but a country cottage routine can be a monotonous one also, and a much harder one.

After this kind of conversation about donkey transport I sometimes resume my journey musing on another aspect of the matter. How about a reversal of the dream? If instead of living simply with little money and a donkey cart I had a luxury flat in town with plenty of money and a car to take me everywhere? Perhaps I will tease the next person with this idea.

"How we envy you," they say.

And I could say, "How I envy *you*!" But no—not even as a joke could I express an envy I do not feel. For in my heart I know that they are strangely right in the way they sense I have something of rare value in my way of life. I am closer to reality, to the eternal nature of life, than I have ever been. Slowing down has caused me to awake within. It is only when we are still that we can *know*.

I am as much a part of life as everything that breathes, and yet in being in it and of it I am also outside it, as a theatre-goer is "outside" the play on the stage. In imagination the theatre-goer is "in" the play, of course, and I am "in" the changing scenes of the hours of the day and the days of the week and the weeks of the month and the months of the years, yet I am also free of this imprisoned pattern. I know that reality is not being hungry or afraid or grief-stricken or over-worked or under-paid or ill or unemployed or tired or lonely, for all these things change in course of time, and what is truly real cannot change. It is there for ever. And reality is not the tiredness of the heart but the sudden flash of joy that will well up in it at unexpected moments, not the wilfulness of the world but the insight into the problem that seeks to find a better way. For me the joy and the insight are there at the heart of things, and the pain passes.

I see a bird wing over the hedge. The sight is a joy. Then I wonder about the winter, and if it will live to see the spring, and about poisonous sprays and whether it will escape them, and if the dwarfed hedges and felled trees will cause a housing problem. But it wings on and on, and every wing beat is a joy, and the joy will not be denied. I know that I am a worshipper of life—the life within the bird—and this life, expressing itself in the body shape of the bird, is the sole reason for the joy. And as this life that is within all things—the roots and the stars and the various body shapes—comes out of timeless regions and vanishes into vistas of eternity, then joy must be the ultimate reality. Of this I am now convinced.

When I went down the deep lane to the sea with Darkie I was not thinking of these things. I was too busy looking around me, reining Darkie in when an extra large car needed to edge by, and waving greetings to people I had never seen before.

At a cottage gate I had an interesting conversation with an old Devon man who remembered helping to build the timber and asbestos bungalow in which we live.

"Fifty year ago, it were," he told me.

"You built it well," I said, thinking of all those Atlantic gales the apparently frail structure has withstood for so long.

The lane turned and dipped and twisted, and we followed it step by step until I saw a flash of silver across it just in front of us. It was a stream, and I was delighted at first, and then alarmed. As it flowed right over the road, to continue our journey we would have to go through it. Pleasantly interesting for me, but I suddenly remembered having read somewhere that donkeys don't like water and refuse to go near it. This meant we would never reach the sea, for I would have to turn Darkie round and go all the way back again. The disappointment was so great that I just sat there with the reins slack in my hand and Darkie, who had so far shown none of my reaction to the stream, which I presumed she had not yet noticed, continued at her same pace towards it.

Any minute now, I thought, we are going to stop. And once she stops I shan't be able to start her again. Then I thought I had better stop her a reasonable distance from the water or I might have difficulty turning her round, and I had no desire to sit for ever at the edge of a stream. At that moment I realised how near we were getting to it. To see what she would actually do was irresistible. I almost held my breath, and consoled myself with the thought that if she came to a standstill, as she surely must according to donkey lore, I might be able to lure her over with a carrot. Failing that I could at least get her to turn round if I got out and waved one.

I remembered seeing a picture of a donkey being blindfolded to cross a bridge over water, and even when pushed and pulled still refusing to budge an inch. And there was not even a bridge here. I suddenly realised that I was soon going to be an object of even greater curiosity than I already was when I went donkey driving! It could be plain embarrassing.

Next minute there was a slight splash. Her front hooves were actually in the water. Surely she had seen it! I waited for a violent reaction as she felt the water. There was none. She continued walking as sedately as before, taking the cart through the stream and safely on to the road the other side. On she went towards the sea.

It was a thrilling moment. Did I possess an exceptional donkey without the inherited fear of her race, or did donkeys vary in their reaction to water? According to what I had read they did not. A mystery indeed, but I was too happy to ponder it. She deserved a carrot for bravery, but it was a pity to interrupt our smooth pace. I decided to give it to her at our first stop.

That stop came as the lane wound down to the sea. As it looked steep I got out of the cart and led her down, after giving her the carrot and enjoying that delicious crunching sound she makes as she eats.

We got down safely, and then to my disappointment I saw it would be difficult to get the cart on to the beach because there was a step. I would have to unharness her.

Watched by an interested small boy, I soon had her free of the cart.

"Would you like to lead her down on to the beach?" I asked this shiny-eyed youngster.

He was shy, but he nodded and reached out a hand to her bridle. Darkie looked at him, then moved off obediently when I told her to while I gathered my bits and pieces from the cart. Following them down, I smiled at the perfect picture they made, the child and the donkey. For surely donkeys were made for children, and there was pride in every upright inch of this child as he led his charge on to the sand.

The sea was a long way out, but I was content to sit just below the path to the beach with Darkie patiently beside me, munching her lunch, and look out into the blue distance beyond the gaily patterned beach—patterned by the scores of family groups in their rainbow colours. Scarcely room to walk between them, and they stretched to where the hot soft sand became flat and firm and damp from the running splash of little waves.

Down at the water's edge were lines of brilliant dots, which I discovered were innumerable children in their colourful, diminutive costumes. Beyond them stretched the unbroken blue of the sea itself—the sea I had glimpsed from the hill to the village, the sea the swallows crossed, the sea in which I with my catarrh should bathe (according to the medical dictionary), but in which I did not even intend to paddle my feet because to me it always feels cold, even on a hot day. But I was there—I had made it. To be there, part of the happy crowd, to know on winter days that I had been to the sea on a summer day was enough to set me warmly basking in the memory of it during the indoor hours.

The small boy stood sentinel to the donkey. He did not ask if he could ride her. Contentment glowed on his face, and he was apparently getting as much enjoyment from listening to her crunching on carrots as I do. He guarded her front legs fiercely from a bouncing beach ball, returning it with admonishing frown to the smaller child who dived after it, oblivious of the donkey in the recovery of his treasure.

I relaxed, feeling pleasantly inconspicuous on that crowded beach. The donkey in the background was part of the scenery, and even people who walked right past us paid her no attention. Not a person on that beach who was not preoccupied—pleasantly so, with the sun, the sea, eating, drinking, buying ice cream, sleeping, talking, playing, child-watching, reading, day-dreaming. It was like a vast outdoor office except that the work was play and there was no time and motion, no tension. Nothing but complete absorption in each individual activity. I, slightly apart, the only person I could see on their own— if I discounted the donkey and the small boy—seemed also to be the only observer. Everybody was too busy doing something to take any notice of anybody else.

It was hot, bright, noisy. I knew I should tire of it soon, but for a time I sat in fascination. A beach crowd, to a lonely person, could appear as indifferent as a street crowd, but here the faces were friendly, even if they did not look directly at you, and lightened with smiles and laughter. There was none of the frowning intensity of street faces. Surely you had but to catch someone's eye and smiles would fuse, or take a step and cheerful words would meet.

I was aware also of the fact that a crowd is made up of individuals, yet the strange thing was that the more I noticed the individuals the greater did my sense of their oneness become. The link was open-air freedom and leisured happiness, and they were all on holiday from their consciousness of the wear and tear of life as well as from daily routine. Happiness is a releasing power, I reflected, and here the outward faces were surely the inner faces, and the inwardness was identical, giving that feeling of oneness.

I stayed a little longer, looking out to where the sand met the sea and then out again over the blue water to where the little summer waves looked snow-capped as their white foam glistened in the sun—out to where the sea merged into sky. In fancy I bathed out there, far beyond the other bathers, out there in the heart of the vastness, all sea and sky, part of the waves themselves— floating effortlessly, cradled and rocked and involved. An ethereal body, of course! In reality I would feel cold, and think of drowning. But in fancy you can do anything, even take a holiday from life.

No, I reflected, physical sea bathing was not for me. I had nearly drowned once. That was a long time ago. It must have been the summer of 1904, when I was ten. There was a fair in a field about half an hour's walk from my home in East Grinstead, and the whole family went in the afternoon. In the evening there were to be fireworks. I was let into this delightful secret, but my brother, Victor, only six, was not told. He was put to bed at the usual time in the large back bedroom that we shared on the first floor of the eight-roomed house our parents rented for seven-and-sixpence a week—actually a high rent for those days, but as the ground floor was sub-let to a Salvation Army captain and ensign we only had to find about half of it. When Victor was asleep— not missing me, for it was not yet my bedtime—we left him in the care of the Captain and adventured out into the dusky summer evening, a rare treat for me.

As this was the first firework display I had ever seen I was both entranced and scared. The fiery lights flashing in the night sky like the occasional falling star I had beheld from the bedroom window were beautiful and exciting, but then they were not actually *in* the sky like the stars. They were not so very high above our heads, and they were falling earthwards, swift and bright like avenging angels. Suddenly there was one that seemed directly above me, obviously its descent designed exactly for my head.

I was holding my father's hand, gazing upwards. Dropping his hand, I took a few steps backwards, still gazing up at the firework. Although I had moved, there it was, right above me. I couldn't have been more certain that it was meant for me if I had seen DAISY written on it in letters of fire, and I turned and fled down the field as if all the fireworks in the sky were hotly pursuing me.

Ahead was what looked to me like a white, dusty road in the moonlight. All roads were dusty white in those days. I ran straight to it. Someone shouted "Mind the pond!" but it was too late. I already had one foot in the water, and it toppled me right in.

I don't remember hearing the splash. I wasn't even frightened. The shock was so great that as the water rose to my neck I felt nothing emotionally at all. I was a religious child, Sunday school being the background against which our lives were built, and I thought I was going to Jesus. In those few seconds I was quite sure I was drowning, and the one thought in my mind was that I must let my mother know I had wanted to say good-bye to her. So I said, "Mum!", hoping someone would hear and tell her.

As my chin went under the water I felt a hard grip on my leg. The man who had shouted "Mind the pond!" had followed me quickly, and my father had joined him. Between them they got me out, and once on the bank I burst into tears. Hush, hush, everyone kept saying, you're all right now, but I felt as if I could never stop crying. I howled all the way home, even though I was being hustled along as fast as my legs could carry me between my parents, whose one idea was to keep me moving as quickly as possible to avoid getting cold.

On the way we stopped at a pub, and I was handed a glass and told to "Drink it up." For the first time I stopped crying. Looking at them solemnly, I asked with great earnestness, "Is it strong drink?" The question was important to me as I belonged to the Band of Hope, and had signed the Pledge. I was well aware that promises were not to be broken, and as I had promised never to touch strong drink I couldn't break my word just because I had fallen in the pond.

They assured me it wasn't strong drink and said it would do me good. As I had implicit faith in the truthfulness of adults I drank it. The hot taste warmed me, and we continued our run home, and I resumed my crying. At home I was given a bath, rubbed down with hot towels, wrapped in blankets, and put to bed, where I remained next day, much to the surprise of my little brother, who then had to be told about the firework display. I was none the worse for my dip in the pond, and on the following Sunday was taken in my best clothes to say "Thank you" to the man who had saved my life.

"Mind the pond!" How plain the words sounded in my ears that afternoon at the sea. Difficult at times to separate past and present when the reaching out of thought brings the past so close that you feel you have but to turn round to see again those you once knew. I turned my head to see the small boy still standing attentively beside Darkie, and knew it was time to go. Gathering up my things, I asked him to lead her back to the cart. We harnessed her together, he quite proud to help, and then he led her up the steep little hill while I walked behind.

When I had climbed into the cart and taken the reins he said good-bye to the donkey, lingered as if he could not bear to leave her, then ran off without a backward glance. Soon he would find a new interest, and the wistful look would be gone. Darkie half turned her head to look after him, then set her nose for home. At a word she was on her way, stepping out at a steady pace.

A horse in a field saw her and neighed excitedly, galloping down to look over the hedge. She appeared not to notice. He neighed the louder, persisting in it, following her along the length of the hedge. Darkie neither paused nor turned her head. He became frantic with neighing. Infuriating for a horse to be ignored by a donkey! Yet lumbered with the cart as she was she went on with gentle dignity as if she had no desire at all to converse with strange horses over hedges.

The road was long, yet she appeared not to weary. Cars from the beach car park overtook her, their owners having stayed on the beach long after we had left it. With tea-time approaching they came almost nose to tail, and we were continually pulling in to the side before one of the many bends to allow them to pass.

Everyone smiled and waved until a van full of children came along. Ugly little scowling faces were pressed against the windows, and words were flung—"Git orf the road!" I grinned. Darkie just went on looking dignified.

As we approached the village the cars were piling up. Soon those ahead were moving as slowly as the donkey cart, and with others crawling behind me I was now part of the procession. On entering the village we all came to a complete standstill.

Traffic jams frustrate drivers and fray nerves—what of a donkey? Without protest Darkie stood there for three-quarters of an hour, completely immersed in herself. She was untroubled by the noise, the panting exhaust of the car in front, and the long wait.

"Enough for the summer, Darkie?" I asked her when, presently, we were free of the village and stood alone on the hill. A brief pause, and then she was on again, climbing towards our familiar skyline which the sun, at a certain moment of setting, turns briefly to silver. It was silver now.

Her ears twitched. Did she say "Yes" or "No" to my question? I smiled knowingly. After a rest in her stable and a few field days she would be as willing as I to be off again. But next time it would not be to the sea. Enough for one summer, Darkie?

Next time we would go to the woods.

D ARKIE likes the green tunnel where the woods begin. So do I. We pause under the great tree branches that form its roof, two shade-worshippers on a day of golden heat. It is solitary here, for the summer visitors are sun-worshippers, and are all down on the beach. Occasionally a car passes through, but the beach seekers do not linger here. The donkey and I have the shade to ourselves.

We have the woods to ourselves too, which is good, for though the beach and the sea and the sunshine give as freely to a crowd as to an individual, the woods withhold their treasure from more than one person at a time.

As we pause in the cool lap of tree shade Darkie browses in the rich summer grass on the verge, the bright green of the blades like an intense joy released from the hidden roots. Where the trees part I glimpse the sky and see a kestrel poised. Sometimes I see a long-legged heron rise from the pond below the bank, a sight that never fails to thrill. Pigeons plunge into the air, thumping on heavy wings, and little unidentified birds flit silently on their aerial pathways. In autumn there are exciting rustles in the hedge and down on to the road come the pheasants, whole families of them, running scatter-brained in all directions, to scramble again on to a trodden grass-way up the bank.

For some time I am content to sit in the cart with Darkie dreamily browsing while I gaze at the picture the woods make—a picture reminiscent of childhood days, for to me these are storybook woods. In the stillness I seem to have turned a page of one of those books—or is it my picture come alive? Yet those great trees with the stature of centuries stand as if engraved on the hillside they cover rather than as living trees growing out of it. I, doubtless, am the spellbound one. Only the air is real as I breathe the fresh morning sweetness of it, gazing at my petrified forest that looks as if it guards a castle.

And the castle is there. A little to the right, dwarfed by the wooded hill, only it is not a real castle, but an ancient manor house. My thoughts go back to a similar house where I was between-maid in 1909 for two bishop's daughters.

This was a happy period of my life, though it began unhappily enough as the result of my father's death and the splitting up of our family. There was no help in keeping the family together in those days when disaster came. Our home was sold up, my father's firm arranged for my little brother to go into an orphanage near London, and the local church people wrote to the bishop's daughters, who lived in Sussex, for a job for me.

My mother went to London to be near my brother, taking a job as housekeeper.

All I can remember now about the parting and my departure for Sussex is falling downstairs with the trunk I had just packed. I was sliding the trunk down when on the third step I slipped, and tobogganed the rest of the way with a tremendous crash which brought my anxious mother into the hall to pick up my remains. I was unhurt, however, as the trunk had broken my fall.

When we parted as a family, each going our separate way, all seemed as rosy as possible in the circumstances following my father's death. My mother had a job, I had a job, and my father's employers had promised to provide a job for my brother as soon as he was old enough. My mother had great hopes for his future as he had been such a bright child at school. But for Victor there was to be no future; for my mother a double tragedy.

Within a year of my father's death she had a strange dream. Later she was to describe it to me as "someone cutting my throat". Next day came news from the orphanage that Victor, who had never had a day's illness in his life, was seriously ill with diphtheria. My mother went at once to see him. His first whispered words were, "Mum, they put a knife in my throat."

It was almost his twelfth birthday, and he asked for a football. On his birthday morning the football was on his bed, and ill as he was, he was delighted. Next day he died. My mother's grief was not lightened until four years later. It was then 1914. Consolation for the loss of her son so soon after her husband came in a flood of relief—"Victor has been spared the war."

The bishop's daughters were elderly and kind. Their chief concern was that I did not know the Catechism,

for although the church people had helped us out after my father's death we had always gone to chapel. I don't think I explained this, being a very shy and nervous fifteen, prepared to say nothing but "Yes, madam", and "No, madam", so I had to bear their horrified distress at my ignorance. This they soon rectified, however, for in between my duties of helping the cook and the house-parlourmaid I was set to learn it. Every Saturday evening a bell rang from the drawing-room and the thin little cook, appropriately named Mrs Small—not a bit as I had imagined cooks looked like, big and robust—gave me a teasing smile with the comment, "That's for you—off you go!" And slightly awestruck I went into the draw-ing-room for a Scripture lesson.

The drawing-room was large with a wide fireplace, where there was always a log fire, and an alcove to one side where a glass chandelier lit by candles was suspended from the high ceiling. There were mullioned windows in three walls from floor to ceiling—hundreds of tiny panes, which were cleaned only once a year.

It was these windows that indirectly contributed to an incident that occurred one dark autumn evening. In the late afternoon there was a knock at the back door. It was part of my duties to open this door, usually to a trades-man. But sometimes a tramp would come, asking for his fare to London, and he always got it from Miss Mary, the younger of the two sisters.

On this particular afternoon Miss Mary was out, and when the old man I had opened the door to asked for her I politely told him so and closed the door. A few moments later there was another knock. It was the old man again.

"Excuse me, Miss," he said, "but the lady isn't out. I've just seen her through the windows."

"That's the other lady," I explained. "She doesn't see anyone. The lady you want *is* out."

He went away. It was already getting dusk, and was soon quite dark. There was another knock at the back door. I picked up a candle and went to open it, having an uneasy feeling that it must be the old man again.

As the door opened outwards the person outside always had to take a step backwards, and my flickering candle did not give enough light to show me who was there this time. But as whoever it was stepped backwards, a stick held aloft shone in the little flame, and appeared to be coming forward to descend on my head. I screamed, dropped the candle, fell over the bucket of coal in the scullery, scattering coal everywhere, and rushed back into the kitchen.

The cook was stirring something in a saucepan. She stopped stirring and stood looking at me with her mouth open, the spoon poised. Then she fled to the hall, and I followed. Here we met Eliza, the house-parlourmaid.

"There's an old man waving a stick at the back door!" I gasped.

Eliza turned white, and ran into the drawing-room. A moment later Miss Otter, the elder of the two sisters, came out.

"What's happened, Ellen?" she asked me calmly. I was always called by my second name, as they apparently thought Daisy not very suited to a between-maid.

Again I babbled about the old man and the stick.

"Where is he now?" she asked, and even in the middle of my fright I envied her that assured calmness of manner.

"I don't know, madam," I had to confess. "I left him at the back door. He might be in the house now."

Miss Otter went back into the drawing-room and returned with her purse. "Give him this," she said, and a small pile of coppers clinked into my reluctantly outstretched hand.

"Please madam, can Eliza come too?" I whispered.

"Eliza can't come now," said madam. "You go along."

My legs felt shaky and I had a terrible sense of injustice, even though it *was* my job to answer the back door, but I went down the passage, through the kitchen and into the scullery, picking up another candle on the way and clutching my handful of coins thankfully as if they were ammunition to save me from the enemy.

As I approached the back door a quiet, amused voice said, "Good-evening, Miss!"

And there on the doorstep stood not an old man with a stick but a young man from the village shop with a new broom he had called to deliver. My relief, alas, was quickly followed by confusion at the mistake I had made. On returning to the drawing-room to report the true facts and return the money, I discovered the reason why Eliza had not accompanied me to the door. She had fainted, and was recovering in an arm-chair.

The laughter at the village shop was long and loud,

and whenever one of us went there it started again. But I was spared further incidents on dark nights, for Miss Otter gave instructions that all deliveries were to be made in daylight in future.

Meanwhile Miss Mary was preparing me for confirmation, and one Sunday I drove to church with her in the carriage, wearing the dove-grey dress she had bought me. In my heart of hearts I had longed for a white or cream dress for this occasion. With the best of intentions Miss Mary no doubt thought grey would be more serviceable for me.

Sitting by the storybook woods in the donkey cart it is easy to remember Miss Mary and the dress and driving grandly along in the horse-drawn carriage. The sight of the big house below the trees brings all the events of those days vividly to my mind, and I sit there enjoying my own private film show. The star part certainly doesn't seem to have been played by me at all, but I share the griefs and joys of that distant girl in the long skirts as I dream under the trees.

"You all right, missus?"

This question roused me one day, and I looked up to see the jolly face of the driver of a brewery van.

I was back in the donkey cart with a bump.

"Fine, thanks," I said. "Just giving the donkey a rest."

He winked. "Sorry I can't stop and offer her a drop."

Sometimes I turn for home without going into the woods. Or I may take Darkie to her tethering place and go for my slow walk along the winding paths. Now is the time for the moment—the moment that I must not miss through going back into the past. I am alive here and now, my senses alert for discovery and enjoyment. I find myself breathing consciously in order to identify the deep scents of the wood, and in the same way listening as if my ear has wakened to catch the smallest sound in the stillness. My eyes respond to the discipline of the observer, and I see consciously and wish that my seeing could extend to the hidden things—down in the earth to watch the activity of roots, the great roots of the trees delving deep for water, the sleeping white bulb roots of the departed bluebells. Or to see the sap rise in the twining stem of the honeysuckle on the hazel.

Lovely are the leaf sprays of the dipping branches, and the tiny stars of flowers in a haze of grass, yet the real delights of the wood to me are its hidden things. A rustle—what caused it? Wind quiver or woodland creature? A black disc of a hole in a split tree trunk—who lies within? What is concealed where the bracken and ferns grow deepest? The wood is full of secrets, and the sense of mystery stirs a response within me. It is like being a child again, and now I find myself wishing that I had gone through life with the open eyes and mind of a child, keeping unveiled the vision and the knowing. But like all who grow up I had also grown used to seeing and being, and the world had lost its wonder during the routine-ridden years. Now I am regaining a little of what I knew as a child.

Not for everyone, perhaps, the peace of a wood on a summer day. Yet to be solitary there is not to be lonely. My mind teems with thoughts and impressions, with fancies and realities. Although I thought of these as storybook woods when I looked at them from the donkey cart they are not only real when I walk in them, but impress me with the feeling that nothing is quite so real as a wood. Here in this community of trees I am aware of life, and never have I been so aware as now of the two aspects, the seen and the not seen. I muse on the unseen element in all things.

Above me is a hidden orchestra. I glance up to where threads of sunshine are spun in and out of the leaves like a gossamer web, but even at that height the innumerable insects creating the rhythmic humming are invisible. None descend to flit insistently around my face, and I walk in clear air and breathe deeply the wood smell, enjoying this all-pervading wood music, enriched at intervals by bird notes.

There among the big trees are the little ones. A fallen acorn in leaf-composted soil, and a root is put down and a shoot up. One small oak tree in particular has grown in perfect shape. Its "trunk" of twig thickness, not more than eighteen inches high, already carries ten small branches.

There are so many inviting places to sit that if I take my lunch—a cheese sandwich and an orange—with the intention of lingering I have difficulty in making a choice. Shall it be on the slope in the slight clearing where the grass is short and thick and bouncy as a foam cushion? From here there is a glimpse of distant woods or small clusters of trees spread like camouflaged armies on the cattle-occupied grassland. A sky view, too. Or shall I sit on the tree trunk in the hollow below the rhododendrons where the trees are as densely packed as a suburban population? Or on the bright cushions of moss among the young hazels? Or shall it be the seat between the low walls of the ruined chapel by the stream?

Sometimes Susy rides with me to the woods. A motionless and dignified passenger in the donkey cart, looking straight ahead, she reverts to the bouncing eagerness of puppyhood again on arrival. She cannot race down the field fast enough, or contain her impatience for me to follow and open the little gate on the other side of the rustic bridge that spans the stream. And once inside the wood she is gone in one single swift white streak, to be lost to sight in the undergrowth, her whereabouts made known to me only by occasional rustles and brief returns to report back at frequent intervals—probably to check that I am still there rather than to show me where she is.

A whistle will fetch her, and we return to the donkey cart at whatever hour I choose. I have only one consideration—to be home before the white rabbit's bedtime.

IT is my task to see the rabbit safely in her shed for the night. She returns to the vicinity of the shed herself at dusk, wherever she has been roaming in garden or field. Often she will go in, but I always like to be there to make sure that she does, and to close the door.

If I return early I may find her on the lawn in the sunshine, even her ears at rest, flat against her back, so that she looks like a snow-covered molehill. Or she may be at the foot of one of the fir trees, tail tucked up to its broad supporting trunk, half asleep in the shade. If I have to look for her I shall probably find her deep among the dahlias, where she has made a burrow, ears, nose and eyes all alert for intrusion from the world above.

Should I be later she will be foraging for her supper, searching out the succulent small leaves of clover and plantain in the long grass in the orchard. Or perhaps on her way to the clover patch in the field, poising suddenly at a sound, body raised, ears high. If undisturbed her movements are leisurely, and she will pause to caress a twig on a low bush with her chin.

When the moment for going in comes I walk up behind her and say, "Home, Bettybunny!" She responds with a rabbit skip—a delightful combination of a jump and a jerk of her back legs, with a flick of her little up-turned tail thrown in. Then begins her favourite game of pretending not to want to go in. She loves me to pursue her, but first makes me think she is going straight in as she runs towards the shed, and then suddenly doubling back, eluding me by diving down a green tunnel of grass, or under a hydrangea. I send her scuttling out, and she leads me in ever widening circles with a skip of her back legs and a toss of those long ears, so like a smaller edition of Darkie's. But I am insistent, and play the game until she lets me win by going home.

When the rabbit is in, the goats in their house, and Darkie in her stable it is time to call the cats. No mean feat, getting six cats in for supper and bed at the same time each night. Their names ring out over the surrounding countryside in which they wander all day, and if within earshot they come. If not, they will come in their own time later. Only rarely does one fail to appear, and then the door of the hay shed is left open for the late-comer if it is our own bed-time, and food and milk placed on the step.

Even with six, each is individual and important, and after dark, if one has not come, I take the hurricane lamp and go down the lane to call again. Sometimes I am answered by tiny distant miaows, and then out of the darkness comes the late one, who always seems flattered to have been "met" and escorted home.

The fact that we have six is more by accident than design. A tight budget has to include plenty of food for them, in addition to Susy's meat and hay and straw for the animals. The fact that it does so is mainly due to Eric, who does all our shopping and is expert at getting quantities of cheap lites and cat fish to eke out the tinned food. With unlimited goat's milk as well the result

is six cats who look to me like cat show champions—
except that they're not aristocratic.

Matilda came first. She "adopted" us, being a very
sociable black puss with a white front, four white paws
and white whiskers. We found good homes for her first
kittens. The second litter caused a problem. They were
three months before a home was found, and the night
before they were taken to the town in a basket to their
new owner they had discovered how to climb a tree and
leap on to the roof of the bungalow. We didn't know
then that the little black one we called Tom Purry, used
to so much freedom, would next day be confined to a
small cage in a pet shop window with kittens much
younger than himself who had not yet learned the thrill
of climbing.

"They only wanted one kitten, after all," Freda told
me when she came home. "I didn't want to leave him at
the pet shop, but what else could I do?"

At that time she was buying only tinned food, and felt
it would have been difficult to stretch the budget to
increase the tins as Tom grew older. All the same she
went down to the village each day to telephone the shop
to find if he had a home yet.

The man at the pet shop said he had been taken out
of the cage and had the run of the shop. But at the
week-end he would have to go into the cage again. On
Saturday I decided Tom *would* have a home. I harnessed
Darkie and set off along the lane to the woods. This time

we went past them, although Darkie lingered at our usual place and needed quite a bit of coaxing to continue. However, once started, she went on.

We followed every bend in the lane until it took us over the hump-backed bridge and out on to the main road. There was quite a lot of traffic. Although used to busy lanes in the summer-time Darkie had never been on a main road before, and I suddenly realised that this was quite an adventure for us both.

Along our lane to the sea all the traffic had been going in the one direction at a steady pace, slowing when they overtook the donkey cart. It had seemed a friendly lane, the narrowness giving an intimate pleasure to the journey. Few people could resist the sight of the donkey, and when the cars slowed the smiling faces made me feel I was one of a big picnic party bound for the beach instead of making a solitary excursion.

Out on the main road it was different, just a blur of traffic coming in both directions, shooting by so swiftly that I didn't even see the occupants of the cars clearly. They saw me, of course, but only fleetingly, and although I would get an impression of faces screwed round to peer through the back windows there were no smiles and friendly waves to return.

How strange it seemed, out on the main road. Darkie behaved splendidly. She was completely indifferent to the cars flashing past her, walking steadily with upright ears as if, being the only donkey on the road, she had to demonstrate her right to be there. My sense of adventure grew. We were on a rescue mission, braving high-powered monsters to achieve it, and achieve it we would.

Yet I knew I could not take her all the way to the town. We would spend the rest of the day getting there, and I could not subject either of us to the busy road for that distance. Or, for that matter, subject the car drivers to our presence on their road.

I mused on the idea of going to town. How long would it take her to cross by the traffic lights? She would certainly wait willingly enough for the green light, but I imagined it turning to red again before she reached the other side. Would a donkey cart cause chaos on the roundabout? Town drivers would be far less tolerant than the beach seekers had been—in fact they would probably be infuriated by the sight of a donkey cart ahead. And how would I park her? Would a traffic warden stretch the limits of his duty and hold her for me, or should I pay for her at the little kiosk in the car park and find a convenient railing to tie her up? In the old days many donkey and horse-drawn carts must have gone to town, and I had a wistful wish that they were all joining along with me on the road then.

At the railway crossing I turned off the main road and went between the crossing gates into our rightful territory—a lane again, escaping the noise and speed on the big road thankfully. I drove to a farm gate, where I tied her while I crossed the yard to the door. No answer at the front—one should always go to the back door on a farm. From the kitchen came sounds of activity. A dog came out eagerly, followed by the farmer's wife.

I explained that I wanted to catch a bus to town, and asked if I could leave my donkey and cart in one of the fields for an hour or so.

While she went to ask her husband I tried to think of an alternative if there was no field available for Darkie. Fortunately the answer was "Yes", and the cost would be ten pence.

It was a nice little field, just off the road. As I shut the gate on her I wondered how Darkie would feel about it. I needn't have wondered. Her nose was already down to the grass. She was certainly a most adaptable donkey, I reflected as I made my way down the road to the bus stop.

I missed Darkie as I sat on the grass verge to wait. There's nothing like your own transport even if it is only a donkey cart. I was still thinking that half an hour later in the same position on the grass verge. The cars roared dizzily past me without a lull as if the road were some giant conveyor belt. Away to my right rose the stream encircled hillside, rich bronze with bracken, tree capped under a sky so blue and bright I thought of heaven.

The cars were like little monsters full of eyes, but what did the eyes see? Not the glory of the hillside. To do so they would have had to gaze with undivided attention, and there is no opportunity for gazing at a single part of the landscape in a fast moving car. The drivers couldn't stop on that wide road, parking for the pleasure of enjoying the countryside. They could, perhaps, turn down one of the inviting lanes that led away from the road into more interesting territory, but none did. The cars were for speed and the speed was to get somewhere in the minimum of time. Everyone was bound for somewhere, even as I was, although I remained seated on the grass verge. I could sympathise with the need to arrive. Even though the hillside held me during my enforced wait, I had to get to that little black kitten, and I wanted to get there as quickly as possible.

The bus came at last, and once on it the journey to town was swift. I thought of Tom all the way, wondering if he was still there, as he had been that morning.

I found him sitting on the counter, looking strangely unfamiliar to me in the shop surroundings—very still and sad, almost automatically turning on the purr when I stroked him. But for this, and the fact that he felt warm, he might have been an ornament.

"He's had plenty of freedom," the man said. "He's been out in the street a couple of times."

As the street outside was jam-packed with traffic I marvelled that a frightened kitten looking for his green acre of home was still alive. But it was not the traffic that nearly killed him, as I was soon to discover.

"Don't be surprised if he's hungry when you get him

home," I was told. "He didn't push in like the others."

He was a kindly man, genuinely interested in the animals in his care, and he had done his best, so I thanked him and went out with Tom snuggled in my coat. As Tom had been a very "pushy" kitten at home I reflected how homesick he must have been.

When I got off the bus near the farm the best part of two hours must have gone by since I left Darkie. There she was with her nose over the gate, looking out for me. I hoped she hadn't been wondering if I'd abandoned her. She had turned right round with the cart behind her, and was obviously all set for home.

We went along at a good pace. Once again I turned off the main road thankfully, into the lane that would eventually lead us past our familiar woods. Tom slept most of the way. He was awake when we reached home, and inside the gate I put him down on the garden path, eager for his happy reaction to being back. Instead he looked round him indifferently and walked very slowly to the door. I took him up and cuddled him, and went into the kitchen.

"Tom's got an owner!" I announced. "Me!"

I never regretted that decision, although it involved us in even more expense than anyone would have expected. After eating a meal Tom went to sleep. Next morning he was sick. He kept on being sick all day, and although it was Sunday we called the vet.

"He's very ill," he said. "I can't promise to save him."

First it was gastritis, then anaemia, coupled with Tom's complete disinterest in being alive at all. Now we regretted ever having parted with him, for he had been strong and healthy the day he left home. The vet came several times, and I saved from my pension to pay him. It was two weeks before Tom showed even a sign of improvement. After that he began to get better very gradually, and in time regained something of his lost kittenhood. By then we had a grey kitten, Fluffball, who stayed with us because he had only one good eye. It was Fluffball who helped to restore to Tom Purry the fun of living.

Homes were found for several more kittens, then roguish black Twinkle stayed because he wanted to, stealing our hearts by pretending he was never going to learn to lap from a saucer however big he grew. Once firmly established in the household he not only lapped but demanded big helpings. His twin sister, Teenie, a pretty tortoiseshell, stayed to keep him company—we might as well squeeze in one last kitten, we said, as we then intended to have Matilda spayed.

The food problem had worked out, and now with five cats and Matilda's operation over we thought we were complete. It was impossible to have any more kittens—or so we thought.

I had quite forgotten that when you go out in a donkey cart anything is likely to happen.

IT was a mild October afternoon when some of the elderberry leaves along the hedges had changed with marvellous individuality, like party-going girls, to pink and amber among the summer green of other leaves. The still air had the warm smell of late blackberries, and there were flocks of starlings on the move, sweeping low over the fields and wheeling up again into a great umbrella.

We paused at the top of the hill, Darkie and I, as we always do. Here I sit back, high above the hedges, and look out across the country. Just below me the sand-coloured stubble of the cleared wheat field stretched to the edge of the woods, its straw bales built up into square stacks like children's sand castles dotting a beach. The woods were a dark green under the pale sky, and on the light green pasture fields black and brown bullocks were grazing. I could see our own white goats in the field below the bungalow, and the bungalow itself tucked in between the conifers. Scores of individual sheep on a high field against the sky suddenly merged into one vast oatmeal-coloured pancake as they were rounded up by the farmer's black and white dog—a sight that never fails to fascinate me.

From this point, too, I can glimpse the manor house again among the trees. I reflect that my best job was undoubtedly the first, with the bishop's daughters. I stayed there eighteen months, much to the amazement of Eliza, the house-parlourmaid, who used to tell me that a between-maid was never kept there longer than nine months, which was regarded as a training period. After that another job was arranged for her so that she could "better" herself.

I "bettered" myself when, eventually, a new position was arranged for me in a much larger household in Surrey. I went as under-housemaid, which gave me a feeling of identity I had lacked as between-maid. Shuttled between cook and Eliza, I had been happy enough, but had not really felt I was anyone in particular. Now I had what I looked upon as a job of my own.

A job of my own indeed! I had no idea what the duties of a head housemaid were, but as far as I could see the one in this household did nothing at all, the under-housemaid (me) being allocated everything. I was seventeen, and I had to work harder than anyone of any age should be expected to work. Peeling potatoes for cook, sweeping and dusting with Eliza, and even taking early-morning cans of hot water upstairs to fill the hip bath for the bishop's daughters was all part of a period of leisure

when I looked back on it. Now I was working hard—
mostly, it seemed, scrubbing flights of stairs from before
breakfast till evening.

My employers were wealthy, and at least eight servants were kept. On Sundays it was compulsory for us
maids to walk two miles to church, and on arrival to
make our way self-consciously up the aisle to the front
pew, under the eyes of the family who would be already
seated at the back of the church, having driven there in
a carriage. All the maids wore bonnets. One of them
whispered to me that this too was compulsory. I had a
pretty little straw hat trimmed with tiny pink roses, and
I remember the hot rebellion that filled me on hearing
this. I made a resolve that whatever happened I *wouldn't*
give up my hat and wear a bonnet.

As it happened I was never put to the test. A month
was as long as I could endure such hard work, and I was
also suffering from frequent nose bleeding. The heavy
meat meals twice a day were more than I could eat, and
I longed for the days of bread-and-butter teas at home
instead of dinner at night. So I looked down the newspaper advertisements, found myself another job, and as
soon as my notice had expired was on my way to St
Leonards-on-Sea.

I continually muse on the old days as I make my solitary way along the lanes in the donkey cart. The smallest
thing will trigger off a memory. Even Darkie herself
brings me close to childhood days, and I find myself

thinking of the horses and van my father drove. I also remember the serenity and security of those days. How small and snug the world seemed. I must have lived in complete detachment from events outside my own home. At nights I would lie in bed feeling so *safe*, making up a "thank you" prayer for that wonderful sense of security, which I interpreted as "Mother and dad and Victor and my home and school and nice meals and playing and *everything*."

Sometimes I wonder if today's children know that same secure feeling. To an extent, perhaps, because given the right circumstances it is easily found within the boundaries of childhood, but not, I would imagine, so completely or in quite the same way, for their horizons are much wider now. And this brings a benefit because the modern generation are more equipped for life than the children of my day—those of us who were fortunate enough to have good homes, and lived such sheltered lives within them.

Even my contact with the Workhouse at that time was a rosy one. As a member of the Young Helpers' Choir I went with the other children to sing at the one in our locality. I saw none of its gauntness and despair—only rows and rows of old people laughing and smiling as they applauded our songs.

I was pondering on security that day in the donkey cart when I came back from the village, thinking that my idea of it in childhood days had been illusory. It was dependent then on certain fixed things, chief among them being home remaining exactly as it was as I had known it from the first hours of my awareness. But that was not possible, since change must come, and when it did come it disrupted everything I had depended upon. In the intervening years I had learned that nothing is secure that is outside of oneself. I knew now that I could lose all and still find within myself a security to uphold and encompass me which the child would not have dreamed possible.

And then quite suddenly, up on the hill ahead of us, I saw a tiny white kitten, just about as insecure as a kitten could be. It was in the middle of the road with cars passing on either side of it. Any moment I expected it to be hit as it zig-zagged about. But the cars went by and it was alone again, running up the hill. I spoke urgently to Darkie, but it was impossible to hurry her. She it is who always sets the pace, and I could hardly expect her to go any faster now we were on the hill.

In the yard at the farm I caught a glimpse of a white cat, but if it was her kitten, as it surely must be, she was quite unaware of its adventures. I became increasingly anxious to reach it, and this seemed impossible, for it was some distance ahead and running away from me all the time.

Then a surprising thing happened. A car coming down the hill slowed, the driver reached out his arm, picked up the kitten, and came down the hill with his arm held out,

the kitten in his hand. As he drew level with the donkey cart he handed it up to me. No words were exchanged. He went his way as if it were the most natural thing in the world to have happened, and I sat holding the kitten, marvelling that I had it safe. Darkie took advantage of the situation to stop and rest.

At the nearest lay-by I tied her to the hedge and went back to the farm. As the kitten was so tiny and had a bad cold I decided to knock and hand it in, rather than leave it in the yard.

Just to cap the unexpected train of events the farmer's wife shook her head when she saw it and said it wasn't theirs. She showed me her own litter of healthy kittens frisking round their basket.

"Oh dear!" I said. "I can't possibly keep it. We've got five at home now."

The farmer arrived and inspected the sneezy scrap in my hands. "Looks rough, that one," he commented. "Not one of ours."

I looked for the white cat in vain. It had gone.

Seeing my perplexity, the farmer's wife said I could leave it in the garden if I liked. But I had a sense of responsibility towards the kitten which had already narrowly escaped death on the road and would surely never survive in a garden, even if its mother returned.

I said I would ask around, but as I went out of the gate it was obvious that so young a kitten couldn't have come far, and there was only one other house near enough to be its home. If it didn't belong there it must have been born wild.

Not expecting much, I knocked at the door.

There were no cats in sight, only a spaniel, so I was not surprised when the middle-aged woman who opened the door said no, the kitten was not hers. Her concern for it, however, was equal to mine as we discussed what to do with it. Even in so small a matter what a difference it makes to have someone else's interest and help. My own concern subsided, and when she shook her head over the state it was in and said it would be kinder to drown it, and she would fetch a bucket and wouldn't mind doing it so long as I stayed with her, I knew what to do. That kitten was going home with me, for the time being at least.

How I got her home I shall never know. She cried and kicked all the way, and my indifferent donkey, who merely cocked an ear occasionally, sauntered leisurely along as if we had all the time in the world.

"Darkie, Darkie, this kitten's *starving*!" I scolded. It had no effect, of course.

When we finally reached home I went into the kitchen and announced guiltily, "I've got another kitten!"

"Oh, no!" said Freda. "I can't possibly manage any more!"

"Tomorrow," I said, "Eric can phone the R.S.P.C.A. when he goes out."

The inspector promised to call. Meanwhile the kitten was taking up everyone's attention. To our relief she was able to lap milk from a saucer, although it must have been for the very first time. There was a tenacity about her, a bright boldness that would not be denied, and even her cold didn't affect her perkiness. She was feather-weight and frail, yet it was obvious she had a firm hold on life, and her miaows were louder than all the miaows of the rest of the cat family put together.

Because of her cold we had to keep her apart from the others, much as we would have liked to put her with Matilda, who had mothered so many kittens. In the day-time I had her in my room, and at night she went across to the chalet in the garden, where Eric and Freda sleep, to be put to bed in a box with a hot water bottle.

Early in the morning she would wake crying, and Eric would come across to warm her milk. Later she would follow him along the path to the house, running close to his heels, tiny tail held high. She was a most sociable kitten, and none of us could help loving her.

We discovered that her little pink ears were full of scraps of leaves and earth. From this we concluded that she really had been born under a hedge and the wind had swept the bits into her ears. Hours were spent cleaning them, and de-fleaing her.

On the morning of the second day Freda announced that she was going to suggest to Eric that since we had five cats one more wouldn't really make all that difference. His answer to that was to write a note to the R.S.P.C.A. inspector telling him there was no need to call.

Next day the inspector came, the note not having reached him in time.

"And how's the donkey?" he asked, for it was he who had inspected the stable and field before Darkie came.

"She's fine," I said. "I'm afraid you've had a wasted journey. We've decided to keep the kitten."

There was no need to apologise. He couldn't have looked more pleased if I'd given him a big donation.

After that there was treatment from the vet for the kitten's cold, which gradually eased. We called her Fairy, and introduced her to the others. This was not a success, involving much spitting and swearing—from the established members of the cat family, I regret to say. It was disappointing to see Matilda, who should have mothered her, also treating her as an unwanted stranger.

Not that she needed mothering. She was completely

independent and self-possessed, and we said she had left her home under the hedge and set off up the hill in order to improve her position in life. This she had most certainly achieved!

In time all the cats accepted her, and she would play

with them, holding her own in wrestling matches although she was only a quarter the size of everyone else.

One day she even went to play with Darkie, and Darkie's response was to roll her lightly under one front hoof like a ball. I quickly rescued her from that game. To my certain knowledge she had had two of her nine lives, if not three, and the rest were too precious to risk.

WHEN I take Darkie to the village post office to collect my pension I think how lucky I am to have all my shopping done for me. Not that I couldn't carry it—there is ample room in the cart —but like some other elderly people I still find the decimal money confusing.

On the way home I reflect that perhaps after a lifetime of practical living there is nothing wrong in becoming just a dreamer in one's old age, browsing among memories or following a line of thought—always provided that one can snap out of it and be alert and interested in the present, and even able to kindle a spark, if not a flame, of interest in what is going to happen next. In a way each day now is more of an adventure than it has ever been, and my interest is often nearer a conflagration than a spark. Perhaps this is because I have the time to think and absorb impressions and give my mind over to awareness now it is freed from time pressures and the busyness of an active routine.

It is no longer I who must practise the little economies, devise meals and organise the household. Thinking of this always reminds me of my third job in domestic service when, escaping from the slavery of the house in Surrey, I went to St Leonards-on-Sea.

The year was 1911. My employers were two middle-aged German women, and if anyone practised economies these two did. They kept three servants—cook, parlour-maid and housemaid (me). It was the exact opposite of my previous job. Here the work was easy—I was always finished by two o'clock—and instead of being over-fed as before I was now half-starved. I spent my monthly wages completely on food.

"That loaf," snapped the cook, when I dared venture a remark about being hungry, "has got to last the week!"

She was well versed in economy. When she made a cake the elder of the two Germans would descend to the kitchen to put out the ingredients. The currants were actually counted. I can't remember the number, but it wasn't many.

They lived on a tight budget because they saved up to go for a holiday in Germany every two years. When I began to get anaemic my mother wanted me to leave, but I was afraid this might jeopardise my next job. I told her the servants would be dismissed when the holiday came, so I would wait until then. No one was more thankful than I when the time came. My mother whisked me off to the doctor, and after three robust bottles of medicine I was myself again—no insignificant-looking little tablets in those days! Medicine was good and strong and coloured, and had a psychological effect that today's tablets lack, for even to look at it made you think you felt better.

My next job was near my mother in London. Again

I was a housemaid, this time in a pleasant household in Kensington, and this was when my romance with Fred developed. He was a hall porter in the same neighbourhood, but I could only see him once a week on my halfday, and for an hour or two on Sunday. This was not enough in the long week—for weeks were very long in those days—so I schemed a way to see him oftener. On some evenings I made the excuse that I had a letter to post. There was certainly a pillar box round the corner, but the envelope in my hand needed no postman to deliver it. Waiting beside the box for five minutes' snatched conversation was Fred.

Far-away days indeed. Dream over them as I may, they will not come again. I never drowse in dream over the fire in my little room, as perhaps befits my age, but always out of doors, in the donkey cart. There under the wide skies of Devon I seem to get a sense of proportion. I can separate dream from reality quite clearly, and, even better, diffuse a reality from the dream. Days that are past may be dreams now, but their essence remains, perfectly distilled in the deep place of the spirit, and the experiences they gave remain part of oneself for ever. For ever? My child-like mind asks "How long is for ever?" And the sky and the earth answer, and my being thrills because there are still untrodden ways. One lives within the day, within the hour, even within the minute, and yet there is a kind of knowing right out into the beyond.

There is so much sky here. There are times when I love it more than the landscape. It seems to reach right down to the earth so that Darkie has only to climb a hill and I might touch it.

I think of a poem I have always liked by Francis Jammes—he who imagined going to Paradise "Upon some festal day of dusty roads" taking with him

    . . . my dear friends the asses . . .
    Whom I so love because they bow their head
    Sweetly, and halting join their little feet
    So gently that it makes you pity them.
    Let me come followed by their million ears,
    By those that carried panniers on their flanks . . .
    God, let me come to You
    With all these asses into Paradise.

How often he must have seen the laden donkeys going along the dusty roads near his home at the foot of the Pyrenees.

Sometimes it is Darkie's past instead of mine into which I find my thoughts adventuring. There is something different about owning a donkey. Impossible to sit in the cart and, looking down, glimpse those two black lines so distinctively shaping a cross on her chocolate brown back without a feeling of wonder. Is it memory that stirs? Sometimes it seems like that—as if I, too, or some other part of me, had some share in those distant events in the history of all donkeys. And Darkie herself? Where was she at that time? Part of the infinite or, even then, a donkey? Perhaps, I tell myself, as children do when they play make-believe, she was that very donkey who must have walked from Bethlehem to Egypt by night.

Dare I imagine a greater moment than the secret journeying of the Child? Sitting up in the cart, I find myself musing about it. So vast and quiet the night, and etched in starlight the solid shadow of that waiting donkey against a stable wall. Light from the window of the inn, perhaps, and laughter—or was it later and everyone gone to bed? Only two figures abroad, warmly wrapped, silent-footed, adding their shadows to the donkey's. One has the radiant face of a young, very new, mother, and the child is warmly snuggled in her arms. She is lifted on to the donkey's back by the broader figure, a man with bearded face. Whispers and reassurances, and the donkey twitches those long, sensitive ears, and the tubby body quivers ever so slightly as the light weight descends. What is she sensing with the weight—a tremor of ecstasy, a shiver of foreboding?

The man is at her head, leading her, and her dainty hooves move willingly, for it was cold standing there in the sharp wind. On then through the night along the winding, dusty road. How slow the journey. Or did that donkey on that occasion hasten her precise little steps? The man would be urging her along, kindly but firmly. They dare not stop, or seek a sleeping place among the olive trees. Perhaps a pause now and then for the donkey's benefit. And then on again, on and on as the sky grew bright with morning and the sunrise flowed over the stars. On into Egypt, and safety.

And that other young donkey who trod upon the strewn palms on the triumphal procession? Never ridden before, yet needing no training, suddenly in the thick of things, unaware perhaps, that all roads were not green with tree branches or tumultuous with cheering people. That donkey, surely, stepped very sprightly along, with uplifted head and quick little youthful steps—how often, as it grew, must it have kicked up those hooves in short gallops over the grass when loosed—and this time loosing meant more movement than it had ever known, its first journey, and its first rider, and from that rider such a sweet kindling flow of life that the donkey had never known in all its youthful ardour.

How much, I muse, did those two donkeys absorb on their historical journeys, and pass down in the inmost spirit of donkeys through the long line of their descendants? At what stage of their existence in time was each donkey born with that mark of a cross? I look at Darkie's large, wise head and wonder many things, and my mental journeys with her span the centuries as we wend our placid way along the lanes.

AUTUMN is hedge-gleaning time. The cutting machine has been down the lane, slicing branch and bramble and wild flower with indiscriminate thoroughness. All day Susy has barked at the activity in the lane, and the cats, tautly poised, in wary curiosity, have kept within the boundaries of home. Darkie and the goats congregated by the field fence to listen to the disturbing sounds, the goats wearing their interested expressions and Darkie with her tall ears upright, like two sentinels.

The long green flowing look of the hedge has gone. It now has a shorn appearance, with twigs like bare bones sticking up, and never a frill of leaf to rustle and sway in the wind.

I do not mourn the lost look of the hedge. The cutting keeps it within bounds, and the growth will be there again in the spring. In the meantime I am too busy to look at it with an eye for beauty. I am looking instead for the gleanings—the fallen sprigs and sprays of leaves that Darkie and the goats will eat. Even when the cut branches have been cleared much is left for a gleaner, and higher up the lane where cars never go, only horse riders out for a gallop, nothing is cleared away at all, and I have a fine harvest.

I take Darkie and the cart up there. She munches away at the feast while I collect and pile the cart—great

armfuls to cast into the field to the eager goats, always ready for a change of diet, and much more to store away with the hay for winter days.

Delicacies indeed! Hazel, oak, willow, elder, ash, beech, honeysuckle and munchy blackberry leaves on long spiked streamers of bramble lying spitefully in the piles of soft grass like primitive weapons of war. How carefully must one go hedge gleaning. I sort and gather, cast aside and make treasured piles of "specials" like the dried campion stems and hazels that have browned and crinkled into biscuit crunchiness. The pale willow leaves for Tim—his favourite—choicest hazel for Snow, oak for all of them and anything and everything for the greedy little one who has grown so fast from kid to goatling. Even the bramble they eat—it is I who have to take precautions against thorns.

Coming back with the loaded cart I remember briefly how the lane looked last time we came that way. A morning of white sea mist at first, with a blueness in the upper air, and then the dancing golden light streaming hazily through until the mist melted away and the lane was lit with sunshine. Every single leaf was wet, and every single leaf shone. No Christmas tree in the world, frosted and silvered and hung with sparkling baubles, could compare with the shining of that hedge. The stars might have changed places with the leaves. And now its morning of glory was gone. Shaved and monk-like it stood in brown winter habit, no leaves now to lend as mirrors to the light. Yet still it remained thick and impenetrable, still within its outer barricades of clipped stems and thorns the soft, clinging grass of the bank and the little tightly-wedged ground plants held the universe of the hedge safe for all inhabitants. Still the little mice and voles could burrow down under the thick warm grass into the leaf composted earth, the myriad insects go their peaceful ways, and even small birds find shelter in the deepest centre. I was more keenly aware than ever of life within the hedge—the life it sheltered and its own pulsing, living roots deep in a hidden universe down inside the earth.

If you cannot take the sensible donkey view, I reflected—that is, to enjoy whatever is under your nose when it presents itself—then to look beyond, above, beneath and around the things that disturb and disrupt and change pleasant, secure patterns into new ways or apparently meaningless jigsaws is the only way for sanity and true understanding. We may not have the full sighted eyes for this kind of looking, but even as we peer in the half-light of strange territory, attempting to marshal our uncontrolled thoughts into the order of reasoned thinking, a little torch may be lit somewhere within us, throwing a beam to follow. In following the light grows brighter.

My slow journeys with Darkie are conducive to this kind of thinking. The journey down the lane with the hedge gleanings piled high around me in the cart is slower than usual. Darkie never neglects what is under her nose, and there is plenty of it here.

Apart from our pleasure trips, she has proved useful like this, not only enabling me to bring home the loads of hedge food for the animals but sometimes fetching bales of hay or straw towards the end of the winter when the supply has dropped low. The first winter I had her, before we assessed our quantities better, I took

Darkie and the cart on a tour of the farms to find a farmer who would be willing to sell me a few bales. It is not always easy to find one, for they grow for themselves. Some years the crop is poor for various reasons, and hay is precious in winter. That year was a winter like that. We travelled miles in the bleak wind making our fruitless calls. Finally I spent a good half-hour discussing the hay situation with a distant farmer, he being disposed to talk if not to sell, and I was hoping that if I stayed long enough I could persuade him to change his mind.

"It's bad nowadays," he said. "We can't even get the labour. The young chaps would rather go off and drive lorries. That's where the money is. You can't blame them."

"It must be very difficult for you," I said, one eye on his huge barn piled to the corrugated roof with hay. "How do you manage?"

So he spent a long time telling me how he managed, or did not manage, and the time involved and the money situation, and the losses, and how if one did have hay over from one season it was wise to hold on to it for the next.

Like gold hay was that winter, he said. Just like gold.

I remarked that right then I'd rather have a bale of hay than a bar of gold. You couldn't feed a donkey gold.

And quite suddenly he said, "Oh, I can let you have one bale."

The deal was done.

After that we had various adventures getting hay, and I paid from one to twelve shillings a bale. The shilling one must have been a gift, that winter of all winters. We had gone to a village we had not visited before, and this time there was no long conversation as a preliminary. A beaming farmer, a bale fetched and hoisted on to the cart instantly, and when I asked how much the reply, "Oh, let's see—a bob will do."

It was no good answering those tempting advertisements in the local newspaper about deliveries of hay. Even if we could have found the money for a ton this was too little to make the journey out worthwhile. It had to be a lorry load, and the lorry, apparently, held much more than that.

However, Darkie and I brought home all the hay the animals needed for the rest of that winter. Since then we have been lucky enough to obtain our winter supply delivered on a tractor by a local farmer.

Darkie and the cart came into service in a different way on another occasion. Eric and Freda had returned from the village with Susy apparently following them. She had slipped through the hedge at the top of the hill and they thought she was running down the field in the direction of home as she often did. Sometimes she was here ahead of them, but that day she was not. By the time they had made a cup of tea she had still not arrived.

The tea was left while they went to search the field

for her. There was already a slight feeling of anxiety. On one occasion, out on a walk across fields, they had whistled her and she had not come, yet when they turned round to look they saw her sitting down under a hedge. They whistled again and walked on, then looking back saw her in the same position, quite still, gazing after them.

On going back to her they found she was unable to move. Her neck was caught in a snare. Wisely she had waited for release. Now there was the dreadful anxiety that somewhere she might be sitting like that patiently waiting again, and would have to be found.

They came back to tell me she was not in the field beyond the hedge. This meant she must have gone further, which was unusual when she was on her way home. While they went back to search the fields I harnessed Darkie to the cart. It occurred to me that Susy might have got out of the field in the lane at the top, instead of the lane leading home, and gone the other way.

Slowly we climbed the hill. It would soon be dusk, but I could still see across the surrounding fields. And there was no little white dog.

We went on, and I took the second lane to the village, instead of the main hill, as they had come back that way. I decided to make a circular tour. When a car slowed to pass me I asked the driver if he had seen her. He had not.

How infinitely precious is the one that is lost. Always the wild thoughts come first—the stirrings of panic in case "something terrible" has happened. I thought of her with the noose of the snare tightening if she struggled, or perhaps it wasn't a snare at all and she had somehow managed to lose herself, was even then roaming in forlorn hope of picking up a familiar scent. She was friendly with people—she could even be kidnapped—picked up by a passing car and sold for vivisection purposes. When I reached this thought I took myself firmly in hand. It was a chance in a million that Susy and the sort of car driver who would do that would meet in one of these lanes. She would be more likely taken to the police station. Panic is an ineffectual state, and I did my best to reason myself out of it. Her disappearance was really extraordinary, and I kept telling myself that she couldn't be far away and that I would find her.

Darkie was walking steadily along, not pausing to eat, no doubt wondering why she had been brought out so late. I hoped we would be back before dark, but had two hurricane lamps in the cart for use if needed. I had no idea how Darkie would react to walking in darkness, but by this time had so much confidence in her good sense and obedience that I knew she would not let me down.

The lane seemed long and empty—so empty because there was no little white dog in it. We were nearing the village now, and my only hope was that I might pick her up on the hill on the way back if she had wandered that way.

Suddenly Darkie stopped, her ears up. I shook the reins impatiently, and told her to go on. She took no notice, except that her ears twitched. She lifted her head high as she does when gazing at something.

"Oh, come on, Darkie!" I said.

Her attention was riveted. At first I saw nothing—and then suddenly there was Susy, lingering in forlorn bewilderment not far from the village shop. I called, and she came, all bouncing joy. I don't know whose joy was the greatest as she jumped up into the cart. And wise old Darkie went on waiting until I was able to take the reins again.

Then home up the hill, with few pauses for she was stable bound. I rejoiced that my intuition had been right. Susy had been led away by scents in the field, left it by the wrong gate and forgotten she was following her master and mistress home, so back she had gone to the village in search of them. How I blessed Darkie for having enabled me to go to her rescue.

ONE day there was a notice in the village about a concert. It took me back years. All the way home with Darkie I remembered another village, a schoolroom, and a crowd of excited children, of whom I was one. It must have been around 1902.

As a member of the Young Helpers' Choir I was taking part in my first concert. My long light-brown hair had been brushed hard in an attempt to give it a sheen it never seemed to possess, and instead of flowing loose and straight as it always did over my shoulders it had been neatly plaited and each plait had a scarlet bow. My cheeks were apple red with excitement when I looked in the mirror, but they certainly didn't feel like the cool apples I picked up in the long grass under our tree. I felt as if I'd been sitting on the hearth at home toasting them along with a slice of bread on the toasting fork.

My thick serge dress had been removed. So had my black woollen stockings and lace-up boots. Yet I was not changing into a beautiful party frock but a long, plain white nightgown reaching right down to my bare feet, for I was to be one of eight "cherubs".

We sang and mimed the action, and to this day I
remember the words of our song.

> Eight little cherubs in nightgowns white,
> Pretty little cherubs with candles bright,
> Two become sleepy and say "Goodnight",
> Two become sleepy and say "Goodnight".
>
> Six little darlings, dear little darlings,
> Bowing low, bowing low,
> Two smile so sweetly and away they go,
> Two smile so sweetly and away they go.
>
> Four little nodding ones, nodding ones, nodding
>   ones,
> Hugging baby tight, hugging baby tight,
> Two scamper off with their candles alight,
> Two scamper off with their candles, their
>   candles, alight.
>
> Two dainty tots with very sleepy eyes,
> Sleepy, sleepy, very sleepy eyes,
> One leaves her mate, who deeply, deeply sighs,
> One leaves her mate, who deeply, deeply sighs.
>
> One little maid with a pretty curly head,
> A pretty, pretty curly head,
> Blows out her candle and toddles off to bed.
> And toddles, toddles, off to bed.

The lilting little tune skipped through my head as we dreamed along, Darkie and I, and once again I was one of the two little darlings who smiled so sweetly—off stage by the second verse, yet still thrilled to be part of it all.

And were we really such cherubs in those days? Childhood for any generation must surely be a mischief-loving time, a time when self-will asserts itself and is liable to collide with adult commands. Rules were stricter then, and made to be observed, and once a command was issued it had to be obeyed. "Go to bed" meant exactly what it said. I, dawdling on the stairs, petulantly remarking that I didn't want to go, had my mother's order reinforced by my father, who came after me with strap in hand. I was up those stairs in no time.

Talking in school also held the threat of punishment. I remember a boy asking me a question, to which I replied with one word, either "Yes" or "No". The teacher saw my lips move. "Stand up, Daisy Crockett!" No explanation was asked for or given—I was simply sent up to report myself to the headmaster.

With what fear and trembling did I regard the big glass panelled door that separated the youngest of us from the large room where the older children were taught, and in which the headmaster sat in state, right at the very end of the room. "Go on!" commanded the teacher. I went out, and walked slowly past the many rows of desks, my head lowered as some protection from all those curious eyes that watched my progress. I had no idea what stern thing the headmaster would say to me, and rather expected to be caned. I stood shakily by his desk.

"And what have you come for?" he asked.

"Talking," I whispered.

A pause, and then, "Go back to your desk and don't do it again."

He probably knew I had already had my punishment in the tortured walk up that long room.

Once I nearly erred in not looking after my little brother properly. I didn't really need my mother to tell me to do this. Being four years older than Victor, I rather enjoyed the sense of responsibility I felt towards him, and usually all that it entailed. I was engrossed in my play that day, however, and when Victor called out to me, "Daisy, I'm falling!" I barely bothered to glance round at him as I replied, "Don't be silly! You're sitting on the ground!"

"I am falling!" he insisted.

I was running after my playmates, but something made me stop and go back to him. "You can't be!" I scolded him. And then my heart bumped in fright. His little bottom was slowly sliding off a wooden board, and his feet were dangling in a large hole. It was the top of a disused well. I was only just in time to save him from falling in.

As his protector I was rather proud of myself one day

for I believed I had saved him from being kidnapped. We were standing in the street with a group of children watching an organ grinder's monkey in a little red coat jig up and down in time to the music and hold out a bowl for pennies. It was probably the first time Victor had seen this, and he was fascinated, his bright little face

filled with wonder. I saw the organ grinder glancing at him. For some reason I felt uneasy. Why should he single out Victor when there were so many of us children in the crowd? Suddenly he leaned forward and said in a hoarse whisper, "Would you like to come with the monkey?"

I was terrified. "Say no, say no!" I whispered in Victor's ear, and scarcely giving him time to say it I grabbed his hand and ran off with him, not stopping until we had reached the safety of our home.

Unfortunately I was not on hand the day Victor found a new game during the few minutes our mother had slipped out to the shop. He must have been about four years old. I was eight, and at school. When I came home I heard all about how naughty he had been. He had taken our father's walking stick, stuck the end in the oil stove until it caught alight, and marched round and round the kitchen, proudly waving the flaring stick. For this he received what my mother called "a good hiding".

We were taught to say grace at meals, just a simple one when we had finished eating. We would put our hands together, close our eyes, and say quite reverently, "Thank God for my good dinner," or whatever meal it happened to be. One day our Uncle Frank was present, and when we had said these words he added, "Please send me a good tea!" I remember thinking he must be rather wicked because he was laughing, and when saying grace I believed one should be very serious and sincere.

Despite the difference in our ages, Victor and I were always close companions. We were together on Oak Apple Day, Royal Oak Day I think it was called, or Chick Chack Day as the children called it. What it commemorated I can't remember, unless it was connected with King Charles escaping death by hiding in an oak tree. At any rate it was the custom to wear a sprig of oak on that day.

Victor and I, on our way to the stables to meet our father, who was taking us for a ride on the van with him, had bare button-holes, and this was quickly noticed by a group of boys who were laying in wait for passing children.

"Where's your chick chack?" they demanded.

Alas, it was too late to pick any then. They set upon us at once, meting out the punishment designed for those remiss enough to walk about on that day without an oak leaf in their button-hole. Our legs were slashed with stinging nettles!

Victor and I each had threepence a week pocket money—and threepence was good value in those days. To earn mine I used to clean my father's boots, and Victor made his pipe lighters. The money usually went into our Post Office savings books. Father brought sweets home for us—we were only allowed a few—and we seldom bought any for ourselves. If we did, we always shared them equally between us, and I still remember going home from school with half a sucked sweet I had been given, to give the half to Victor.

During my last year at school I could have taken an examination to pass on to the next, and last "standard", as the classes were called. If you passed you "went up", if you failed you stayed where you were. As I had passed each time, I was now afraid that this last time I would fail. So I didn't sit the exam. When I left school at fourteen I stayed at home to help my mother until one day my little brother came in to say his schoolmaster had asked the boys if any of them had a sister who would like a job helping the master's wife. This became my first job, and I was paid half a crown a week for my help in doing the chores and wheeling the new baby out in the pram—called a mail-cart at that time. I felt very proud wheeling the baby along, and used to take him home to show my mother.

I still recall my father's words when I arrived home with my first week's wages. "Now you can keep that, and next week you'll have five shillings, so you can buy yourself a pair of boots."

And that was what I did with my first two weeks' wages. We always wore lace-up boots, never shoes, in those days.

On Sunday afternoons, Victor and I always went to Sunday school, and on Sunday evenings in the summer we all went for a walk, dressed in our best. We lived in a number of places owing to my father's work, and wherever we were walking in the country was our main relaxation as a family. One well-remembered walk was when we lived in a little village near Aldershot, and while we were out we saw Queen Victoria reviewing the troops. That was not a Sunday, of course.

The Sunday walks I remember best were at Dorking. We would walk two miles to Box Hill, our parents stopping at The Punch Bowl for a drink while we played outside. It was on Box Hill that I first made the acquaintance of donkeys. They were right at the top, giving children rides one holiday time. How excited we were, and how we loved them. They looked so miniature after the big horses that drew our father's van. I would dearly have liked one for a pet, but I knew that although rabbits were permitted in the back garden a donkey would not be. So the desire remained a secret dream, to be realised seventy years later.

When I am thinking over all this in the donkey cart along a quiet lane I may suddenly "wake up" and find that Darkie has stopped. Not to eat, not even to rest, for there is no reason to do so when we are not on a hill. Like me she seems to be just dreaming, her tall ears at slightly different angles, her large eyes looking at nothing, her body in repose between the shafts. A day-dreaming donkey, and in the middle of a journey, too. But who am I to chide her? There are indeed a pair of us, drowsing in warm air, motionless, enclosed for the time being within ourselves, looking, no doubt, like last-century travellers carved on the road.

I flick the reins with a gentle word for her, and as we move on again I think what a pity it is that I cannot impart my thoughts to her, nor she to me. For I would love to know what she dreams about.

AFTER the hedge-gleaning the weather changes. There is a new sound in the fir trees that we have not heard all summer—the sound of wind. I lay in bed at nights and listen, and picture the branches sweeping the air like feathery green brooms.

Gone are the sunshine days of warmth and stillness when Darkie so often selected the patch of dry earth to roll on like a ludicrously large kitten, her four strong legs in the air, and the baby goat stepped faun-like down the field to watch. Now the animals are more often close to the hedge than out in the field. No longer do the three goats sit in a row with their backs to the sun, Darkie in her motionless standing position behind them, upright to her ear-tips, as if on guard.

As I listen to the wind I see the picture again, as I so often saw it in the summer. The goats had an air of great concentration as they sat there, ears at the angle of aeroplane wings in contrast to Darkie's skyscrapers. No longer even chewing, they would gaze straight ahead, apparently at nothing, reminding me, of all things, of three monks at prayer. And yet perhaps it was not so incongruous. Their serenity in the presence of each other, their comfort in the soft grass and enjoyment of the sweetness of the air and sun was, in a way, a prayer in itself.

Now they do not even indulge in their more light-hearted activities, with Darkie referee at a butting match between the baby goat and the big billy—father educat-

ing son in the use of horns. Tim has a massive head-piece, three inches wide at the base, curving over his head and tapering to fine points. Against these dun-coloured monstrosities of bone—or spectacular headgear, whichever way you like to look at it—beautifully silvered by sunlight, Frisky's little white crinkly horns, straight upright and not eight inches high, would click again and again until, with closed eyes, one might imagine swords flashing as a duel was fought in the field. But this would be no fight, just the mildest of play, with Darkie looking on in calm interest. Should the duellists move any nearer to her—for Darkie always kept at a safe distance—she would turn her broad rear towards them, and a bowing head in her direction would be greeted by sternly meant backward kicks from her two hind legs, these being her personal equipment for protection, apparently specially designed to keep butting goats at a distance.

But summer play is not for the windy autumn days. Now is the time for more serious food foraging, the grass in the field having lost its flavour. Beneath the hedge it is still long and green, and there are bramble and thistle and fallen leaves to be found. The hedge also provides protection against the weather, and there throughout the day they will linger until the goats tire of it and find a way into the orchard for a feast of blown apple leaves and stinging nettles. Then they have to be tied on short ropes to keep them from damaging the trees.

Deprived of their company, Darkie stands in lonely dejection for a time, then comes to the field gate and gazes through. Not for her the secret exits of the goats. Her size demands a gate, and that thrown wide. They can climb a bank, duck beneath barbed wire, squeeze through the smallest gap, and take the greatest delight in this agility. She must wait at the gate till someone comes, and if no one comes she will throw back her head and bellow her summons for attention, not identifiable as a straight-forward "hee-haw" but beginning as a magnificent roar that one of her ancestors must surely have learned from a lion, and then unfortunately severing all connection with royalty by tottering down several tones into a squeaky wheeziness as if her voice wants oiling.

The goats tolerate being tied for the sake of the feast, but Darkie dislikes it, and unless the weather is too bad or it is time to leave the field she is consoled by biscuits and carrots and a pile of hedge cuttings. Left to roam at random in the orchard she would eventually end up on the vegetable plot, but on her way to the stable she has her set routine and can be trusted for ten minutes or so. Then she will make her way to a particular apple tree and rub herself—slow, long, satisfying rubs, from the expression on her face ecstasy for a donkey. Suddenly she will change her tree for one of the firs, and the rubbing is repeated until someone appears with her food bowl, which she will obediently follow into the stable.

If we venture out, Darkie and I, on a day that is full of wind we make our way down the snuggest lane we know, to the woods. And then I find that even the wood is filled with wind where the big trees are, and I walk in the cool stream of it, watching the delicate dance of the ferns still green beneath them. I soon turn, however, to seek the denser, bushy part of the wood where I can walk in the luxury of summer calm on this wind-blown autumn day.

I tread upon a soft path of pine needles, thick as a carpet. Small leaves drift down like coloured snowflakes, but the large leaves of the Spanish chestnuts are not yet released from their twigs, and glow vividly above me, not unlike crinkly yellow lanterns.

Sometimes in the late afternoon the wind changes. Here the weather will do innumerable quick changes, sometimes within minutes. I have sat warmly wrapped in sunshine looking out on fields golden with it, not a hint of change in the air. Then far off there is a slowly moving whiteness, as if a puff of cloud had fallen out of the sky. Nearer and nearer it comes, and I watch fascinated, listening to strange sounds, as if an unearthly orchestra is tuning up within it. When it is only a field away wraithlike strands of it begin to float into our field, and with them comes a coldness. A perfectly ordinary afternoon in open country suddenly ghost-haunted? I shiver slightly, but it is only the sea mist creeping inland, and bringing the gulls. Their cries fill the air, yet they remain invisible, and the garden also gradually disappears from view as the mist fills it. I go indoors, and looking out of the window we seem to be snowed up. In the room there is that strange sense rather than sight of whiteness that snow gives.

The mist may remain an hour or two or be gone within minutes, restoring the garden and fields to the sun. I have turned from the window unable to see out for mist, and within two minutes have looked again and it has quite gone, and there is the view, as if the mist had never been.

On those afternoons when the wind changes direction and there is an iciness in it the noise in the fir trees is tremendous. It is a roar that comes only from the north. Usually this north wind changes again without bringing snow, but while it lasts the noise seems to increase in volume all the time. I marvel that the house itself is not devoured by this monster of a wind, for it seems as if something alive is attacking the fir trees and bearing down on everything in its path. How thankful I am when the animals are snugly bedded down for the night, and we within doors behind drawn curtains. Even then I never sleep until the wind has gone.

Darkie dislikes wind and rain, but she prefers the shelter of the hedge to going home too early to her stable. Only when rain is heavy and persistent will she welcome the opening of the field gate.

On wet days my room is a haven for the cats. They seem to regard it as a kind of inner sanctum, and when the kitchen has served its purpose for meal-time they make their way to my door, which they push open. Doors always have to be left ajar when there are cats— that is, unless you wish to be free from interruption. On such occasions my door remains closed, but on wet days I seldom disappoint them. I haven't enough chairs for all these visitors, but they quickly accommodate themselves on the dressing-table, top of the wardrobe, the foot of the bed, and before the fire, my lap being favourite, of course, but unfortunately not large enough for all six.

And then after the rough, wild days of wind and rain on this journey through the year there will be a haven of a day. So still and soft, it seems to enclose the garden in gentle arms to compensate for all the buffeting. Then it is a pleasure to walk the paths, to pause under the trees, to watch the animals in the field. It is also the time for Darkie and me to go out again before winter is upon us.

I long for a mild December so that we can go out just before Christmas to gather holly and ivy. And which will be more real if we do—the gathering for *this* Christmas or those long ago Christmasses which try to steal the scene again in my mind? Sometimes it seems that past and present blend, and all is one.

Jogging carefree along that first year with Darkie, I remembered those childhood days. How, on Christmas Day, my mother would draw the curtains in the front room and we would sit in this unaccustomed darkness in the middle of the day experiencing the most delicious tremors of excitement. Suddenly the door was thrown open and in would come the Christmas pudding, borne aloft by my mother. It didn't look in the least like a pudding, though it was perfectly visible in the darkness. There it was, blazing away with a lovely blue flame. My mother had followed the old custom of pouring brandy over it and setting this alight. The result was thrilling to us children, though I was always disappointed when the flame went out, the curtains were drawn back, and we sat in the dull December daylight to eat that magical pudding.

There was more excitement to come, though. Again drawn curtains, and this time it was a bowl of muscatel and almonds that was set alight. In its way even more thrilling than the arrival of the pudding as we had to dive our fingers quickly in and out of the flame to grab as many "trophies" as we could.

The drifting coloured leaves reminded me of the delights of Christmas on that autumn drive with Darkie. The day was damp and grey, the hedges and the fallen leaves sodden after rain the day before. And as the coloured leaves fell on the sombre unidentifiable leaves underfoot I felt a sadness because as the years pass Christmas loses its magic.

A blue flame on a pudding would intrigue me no longer—it would take more than a struck match now to kindle an answering spark within. Yet perhaps it is not so much that we grow beyond simple things—it is, after all, many simple things that thrill me still—as the fact that consciously or sub-consciously at Christmas one not only looks for something beyond the ordinary but tends to mentally discard anything that merely masquerades as Christmas. One is looking, perhaps for *the real thing*. And what is "the real thing"? Maybe the measure in which we find it is the measure of our development within ourselves.

I reflected that my mother's happiness at Christmas had not been because of the blue flame on the pudding but because she, by conjuring up the blue flame, had contributed to our happiness. That is the way it goes, as most people discover at some stage in their lives—in giving happiness to others one receives happiness. And yet it seemed to me then that it wasn't so much a matter of happiness. There are times when one seeks even beyond happiness, and an adult's Christmas is one of those times.

It is not the rose we want, but the scent of the rose—and how to take out the scent and say *"This is it"*? The bottle of perfume may be there, but like the trappings of Christmas it is not the real thing.

As usual when I reflect and dream Darkie too had stopped to dream. I smiled and shook the reins, and she, with a shake of her ears, sauntered on. As I looked down at her I caught myself wondering if, this year, that donkey would in some way help me to reach the inwardness of Christmas.

I had never spent Christmas with a donkey before.

I WOKE to a November morning of sun-topped mist. From my window I watched the fields slowly uncovered, as if a bed was being stripped, and saw the trees emerge. Tall grass stems had little white flags of mist at their tips, the tops of bushes were strewn with tangled skeins of it like thick grey mending wool, and the open squares in the pig wire fence between field and garden had been filled in with lighter, silkier strands that glistened.

When I went down the lane I saw that the sombre hedge, too, had been dressed by the mist, and the sun was setting a sparkle on every twig. I walked down the lane and back for the pleasure of seeing this unexpected beauty of the cut hedge.

The sun promised a golden day, and I reflected that my favourite time of year could well be November. Grey its reputation might be, yet it could produce such a day as this—a day not only reminiscent of summer but possessing a freshness and sparkle that summer days can never give. The very rarity of the day made it precious and worth a hundred others. If November produced only one day like this in the whole month I would rather be alive on it than all the days of summer.

I decided to harness Darkie and drive to the Straight Wood. We call it that because it is a wood almost entirely of firs. I tied Darkie on the outskirts, where the trees have been felled. The sun was now so warm I nearly left my coat in the cart, but decided against it as I was going out of the sunshine. The wood is dark and deep. The firs grow so closely together, and to such a height, with all their green branches at the top, that not a sunbeam penetrates. Somehow it is daylight, but no more than the light in a room through drawn curtains.

The path I walked on was so deep in the dropped needles of the firs that I could have dug up bucket-loads of them. I could almost feel the pressure of the trees around me, on either side of the path, as if I walked through a crowd of people. They enclosed me with a feeling of great friendliness. It is a very friendly wood, with an openness between the trunks of the trees although they appear to grow so close—that is, the base of each tree is free from undergrowth. A low green plant carpets most of the wood, looking as if it has run happily all over the flat ground, unrestricted by any other growing thing. On the further side, where the light flows in more freely from the open field that runs the length of the wood, the ground ivy shines so brightly it could almost be mistaken for flowers. No ivy has ventured to climb the tall, clean trunks of the firs.

I went, that day, to my favourite place on the furthest edge of the wood where other trees grow. Here there is an impressive mound, quite high and long, reminding me of an altar. The "candles" are three chestnut trees. Beside it slopes an enchanting hollow, like a cradle, and it is soft and sweet with very bright green grass.

And then I saw the young sycamore trees that form the hedge between the wood and the adjoining field. They blazed with gold. It seemed as if every leaf had changed to exactly the same colour at the same moment. I don't know how long I gazed, but suddenly I was hurrying out of the fir wood to go to the woods beyond the stream, for it is important in autumn—as, indeed, in spring—to go to certain places at exactly the right time if you are not to miss any of the beauty. And there is a time in a wood when that first hint of changing colour, with varying tints here and there among the trees, becomes a whole tableau of colour to which every tree contributes. So it was that day.

I walked the highest path of all and looked down through canopies of golden leaves to the black and white cows far below the roots of those trees in the green field beneath the wood. Then I searched until I found the most beautiful tree of all—a beech whose leaves had reached a shade of orange-brown, yet were still inter-mingled with green.

Under the big trees the leaves were falling gently—sometimes just a single leaf, then two or three, and suddenly an exciting rustle in the topmost branches followed by a whole shower of leaves. Silently they fell, floating, spinning a little, to lay their brightness on the piles of leaves already fallen. Some never reached the ground at all, and as they settled on the high green branches of a fir they looked exactly like oranges growing there.

I watched a single leaf float down and tried to capture the feeling of being released from a mid-air twig where life had been a firm anchorage—a twig on which you had your little flutter with the dancing wind without leaving the parent home. How pleasant up there, surrounded by all the other leaves yet feeling the air around. Part of the changing day, from rise of sun to star-shine and deep night; part of the weather too, and nothing to do but *be*! If a leaf had awareness—and who can say to what extent the life spirit flowing up from the great tree roots into its tiny stem and veins and body fabric arouses a kind of awareness within it?—then might not the fact that there were no wearisome activities to divert produce that *knowing in stillness* which even the human heart, for all its high estate above a leaf, has difficulty in attaining?

Such were my reflections as I watched the leaf twirl unhurriedly down. What controlled the moment of landing? The line of descent one would imagine, unless a wind came and blew it off course. But no wind came, and at the last moment that leaf deviated from its aerial pathway which had been almost straight, allowing for a few leaf twirls, from high twig to within a foot of the ground. Then it floated gently sideways so that instead of falling on the path on which I stood it drifted close to the broad trunk of the tree from which it fell. I indulged the fancy that the leaf itself had controlled this movement, seeking the shelter of the tree that had reared it, to return, in course of time, direct to the mother roots and so avoiding the risk of merely being trodden into the unyielding path.

I was still looking at the golden leaf nestling against the grey trunk when a small voice behind me said, "I saw your donkey on television."

A little boy stood there. He couldn't have been more than four, and I wondered how he had got there, right in the middle of the wood. I realised how deep in thought I must have been not to have heard him rustling through the leaves. Because a small boy like that would surely have rustled very loudly indeed.

"Hallo," I said, smiling at him.

He had a solemn little face, and looked at me gravely.

"I'm Gerry," he announced.

"Hallo, Gerry," I said. "What's your other name?"

"Gerry-dunno-who-I-am!" he squealed, roguish laughter breaking out all over his face.

"Would you like to see the donkey?" I asked.

"I seen her," he said. "I bin talkin' to her. So then I thought I'd come and find the donkey lady."

"That's me," I nodded. "Where do you come from, Gerry? How did you get here?"

"Boys," he said, jerking a thumb over his shoulder.

Faintly across the wood came the ring of voices. They

sounded a long way off, but were unmistakably boys shouting to each other.

"And how," I asked him rather severely, "do you think you're going to find them again? Among all these trees?"

He was not even listening. I soon discovered that it isn't always the children who ask the questions. Gerry didn't ask anything. He simply told me things, as if he knew everything. I was the one doing all the asking.

"I told your donkey a secret," he announced.

I took his hand and began walking in the direction of the voices. "Do you think she'll keep it?" I asked.

He was scornful. "Donkeys can't talk."

"Not even to other donkeys?"

Was he alarmed, momentarily? The look fled, and he declared stoutly, "It's a donkey secret. All donkeys know. I told her I knew too."

I wasn't going to ask to be told because inviting the confidence was likely to have it refused, but I hoped he might tell, for it was a fascinating conversation. Instead he just went rustling through the leaves and said nothing at all for a few minutes.

Then he said, "If there's an angel in the road going home you won't be able to get by."

"An angel?" I asked, puzzled.

"Yes," he said. "You won't see it but the donkey will because donkeys see angels."

"Do they?" I asked, feigning surprise, for I knew my role by now. He was the one with all the information, so I wasn't going to spoil it by telling him that I was now remembering the Bible story from which he must have got his idea.

"Yes," he said triumphantly, and then bubbled into his story. "There was this donkey, see, an' it went off the road into a field, an' the man hit it an' it went back again, but the road was narrow an' it went close to the wall and hurt the man's foot, an' he hit it again an' it went on, an' then he hit it again because it suddenly fell down, an' he couldn't understand it, but the donkey spoke to him because there was an angel standin' there an' give it a voice, and then the man saw the angel too, an' he was sorry."

"Good gracious!" I said. "I hope Darkie doesn't meet an angel, or I'll never get home."

"She won't," he said confidently.

The shouts of the boys were nearer now, and when I saw them coming towards us I let go his hand.

"Off you go then," I said. "Good-bye."

He lingered. "I wanted to find the donkey lady."

"I am the donkey lady."

"I want," he said, and stopped.

"You want a ride in the donkey cart?"

He shook his head. "I want it to be Christmas. It's nearly Christmas, an' I want it to *be* Christmas." A pause, and then rather shyly, "I want to see your donkey kneeling in her stable on Christmas Eve."

As he looked at me earnestly I tried to find the right words. "Yes, I know what you mean. It's a legend about the cattle, isn't it? You know, a story."

"On Christmas Eve they all kneel down," he said.

"Well, perhaps," I said. "It's very late, you know. Midnight. You'll be asleep then."

"I want to see!" he insisted.

The boys were calling him.

"Off you go," I said. "If I see you again we can talk about it."

His solemn little face broke into a big smile.

"See you Christmas Eve!" he shouted, and ran to join the others, kicking up the leaves as he went.

The voices went ringing through the wood. The echoing laughter and cracking of twigs sounded strange, for usually the woods are silent and undisturbed. I stayed under the big trees and listened till they had all gone, till the last faint shout had dissolved in the distance and no more echoes came. Even then I stood a few moments longer, until I became aware that a chilly wind was creeping through the trees.

I went back to Darkie, eager to drive home. You should never linger after the enchantment has gone.

D AYS of misty, drifting rain followed. Golden November had gone, reverting to the traditional grey. I reluctantly abandoned any attempt to go out with Darkie, confining my outdoor activities to feeding the birds and looking after the white rabbit, in addition to visiting Darkie in her stable.

The rabbit had had a good summer, living the endless hours of her free life in the garden in the various ways she had devised for herself. Sometimes she had been on the vegetable plot, moving from one delicacy to another. A nibble of spinach, a pea leaf, parsley. We called it her supermarket. Fortunately for us everything survived except the carrots. She took the tops of these when they were half an inch high, and their lacy green leaves trimming the patch of loam black earth were gone within days. Gaps appeared at first, like holes in the trimming. Then there were no more gaps—just the untrimmed earth where she had eaten her way along.

Summer mornings had found her lingering in the orchard. She would dart in and out of sun and shade and immensely enjoyed concealing herself. In the after-

noons she would be out on the sunny lawn, boldly crossing to and fro in front of the house. Sometimes I would
see her poised in mid-run on raised body, ears high. Or
she would move leisurely, pausing to caress a low bush
with her chin in a gentle, rubbing movement. I always
maintained this was a gesture of pure love. To me she
seemed in love with the earth—the feel and the smell of
it, the things that grew in it, even the air enclosing it.

Summer had been her paradise. A paradise of sun-
warmed air, cool green undergrowth, long outdoor
hours, and a feast spread on the banqueting earth beneath
her feet. And now that summer had gone she still insisted
on an outdoor life, coming out of the shed every morning and going her way in the garden. Her only conces-
sion to the weather was to alter her habits. She always
had her set places. On a windy day I would find her
behind a tree trunk, facing away from the wind. In a
gale she would be in the deeper security of bushes. For
rain shelters she chose a hedge or a conifer.

Whatever the weather she would never return to her
shed till dusk. I remember when the white mist came up,
gradually enclosing all things within it. She was sitting
against the rockery. When the garden was awash in mist
and the trees had disappeared I thought she had gone in.
But she was still there, invisible until I almost stumbled
over her.

I go out at certain times to give her brown bread. This
always brings her scurrying to my feet, and she snatches

the bread with an eager little grunt of satisfaction. In her thick white fur with its big "collar" round her neck she looks snug enough for the hardest weather. It was that collar of fur, giving her so regal an appearance, that reminded us of pictures of Elizabeth I in high-necked ruff. So of course we called her Elizabeth, and of course it eventually became Betty and finally, bereft of all dignity, Bettybunny.

The birds dash to my window to ask for food, so out I go again, not forgetting a carrot on the way for Darkie. If Darkie is "at home" I am not allowed to pass her stable without stopping. She hears my chirrups to the birds, which brings them flocking, and loses all interest in her hay net. Out will come her broad face, soft nose questing for a tit-bit, and if there is no hand in which to push that nose with gentle firmness she soon lets me know. An ear-splitting summons is always an imperative one. So I go.

Thus I whiled away the rest of that November when we seemed to be living between white walls for days at a time, our field and garden being enclosed in mist. There was also my indoor "greenhouse" to tend. I had picked the half-ripe strawberries from the elevated strawberry plants which fruit till late in the year, and put them in jam-jars by the window.

How much one can have and do in one room! Here are all my treasures. I have books and sewing and radio, a comfortable chair by the fire, an oil stove on which I can boil a kettle, cats in and out, birds at the window in winter and roses in summer. From one window when I look out I can see Darkie looking over her stable door if she is home and the fields to the skyline, and from the other the goat pen and garden.

That room was a little world in itself on those November days when the mist outside walled off the view. It felt secure and serene and self-contained. Although I would not like it always to be so, I gave up wanting to go out for the time being, and adjusted to the indoor routine, to being busy and interested within the four walls. Our only excitement was when the little red Post Office van drew up at the gate with letters. I watched for the post because one of my interests was doing newspaper competitions. One day I would win— or so I thought! Apart from this the post here is always exciting, for we not only wonder who has written but enjoy seeing the postman. He and the oil man are our only callers.

So the misty days slipped away in their strange soft silence, and then the rain came, drubbing noisily on roof and windows, dripping stealthily from the half naked trees, splashing in the water butts, oozing into rivulets on the muddy paths. Darkie and the goats stoically went under the hedge in the field for a short time each day, going in early for brisk rubdowns, hay and dry beds. How well they accommodated themselves to the weather, I reflected. Unperturbed, placid, friendly, as brightly aware as ever, their behaviour expressed no rebellion.

And after the rain there came pale washed skies and a tender sunshine that was sweet to the uplifted face, and in the shady places air like a mountain stream, fresh and clear. Just before Christmas I harnessed Darkie for the last time that year and we went on our holly and ivy trip.

The approach of Christmas had come almost unnoticed. No bright shop windows out here to remind us, no jostling, laden shoppers, sparkling Christmas trees, coloured lights and compliments of the season. We could almost forget the Christmas season but for the extras coming home from the town bit by bit in Eric's haversack—mincemeat, fruit for the pudding and cake, dates, jellies, a present or two for people we know.

But that, I reflected, was the festive Christmas. Out here it should be possible to find the reality—surely a reality as real as the shine on the holly leaves, as bright as the glowing berries. Yet the leaves shone and the berries glowed whether it was Christmas or not. Whatever atmosphere was generated among the fields and trees and under a sky full of stars at night was generated always. I could walk out in any fair weather on any morning or afternoon or after dark and find it. Nature knows no Christmas date, only the date of leaf bud and fall, of flowering time and harvest. If I looked for a visible sign I would not see it.

I could not cross the fields to church on Christmas Eve, but perhaps I could listen for the bells from my window. A night of stars and bells, a donkey in the stable—might not these be the outward things that could transport me to the inwardness of Christmas? The bells would sound very sweet and far away, if their sound came at all, which would depend upon the wind, and if the weather were clear the stars would be thicker in the sky than pins in a cushion, the low ones very bright. It could be like that on a hundred nights, except for the bells, yet because it was Christmas I would think and feel in a different way. That, then, was the secret, and atmosphere had little to do with it. Perhaps one should even withdraw from atmosphere, which is still part of the outwardness of it all, and retreat within oneself.

On Christmas Eve I went to say goodnight to Darkie as usual after tea, taking her biscuits and carrots. This nightly ritual is completely familiar to her, and she rattled her door when she heard my step. I set down the hurricane lamp and unfastened her top door. Out came her nose, soft and questing, her ears on tip-toe with expectancy. We eke the biscuits out with conversation and nose pats—I do the conversing and she listens and thrusts her nose at me if I'm too long about the biscuits.

So it was then. I let her rub her chin on the bottom door—that slow, satisfying movement that she loves. She will do this on the end of one of the shafts on the cart too sometimes. Nose out in the mild night air, slightly damp because of a hint of rain, she continued her ecstatic rubbing, dark eyes deep with their dreamy look. I gave her another carrot and closed the door, thinking that I might come out again later to see if the clouds had gone, and to listen for the bells.

I was sitting drowsily over the fire in my room when the time came. Instead of going out I opened the window. The air was sweet and soft, still damp, but a patch of sky had cleared and my favourite bright stars hung low, as if they were not far above the top of the hill. Faintly across the fields, so faintly as to be almost dream-like, came the sound of the bells.

As I leaned on the sill listening I became aware of another sound. It was unmistakably the squeak of the gate. My first reaction was surprise. Freda and Eric had gone over to the chalet to bed. Callers are almost unknown here, and who would call so late? A feeling of alarm was replaced by logic. Possibly, I thought, carol singers had come. I remembered other Christmas Eves, so many years ago, when I would always lie awake on this magic night of the year, listening—not for Father Christmas, but for the carol singers, who came late and whose voices sounded very sweet in the darkness as they floated up to my bedroom. That was the moment when I *knew* it was Christmas. It was never again quite so much Christmas as it was then, not even when the pudding was set alight.

But this time there was no singing, and suddenly I

knew there would not be. It was most unlikely that carol singers would call here at that hour, visiting one lonely house in the fields. It was that word *lonely* that alarmed me again. Whoever had opened the gate had not knocked at the door. I closed the window hurriedly. I was shaking, and told myself to stop it. But imagination had already taken over, and as I listened I was thinking of the lock being forced, or a window broken, and a burglar in the house. Then Susy barked in the kitchen, and went on barking. The relief was tremendous for the moment. Surely, I thought, no one would break into a house with a dog barking.

The only thing to do was to feel safe—to feel protected. I shut my eyes and prayed like a child. The intense feeling I put into this removed all fear. Calmly I went to the other window in the bedroom to look out, first of all placing the oil lamp which lights my room in an alcove, and shading it so that the room would appear in darkness from outside.

I looked cautiously round the curtain. Through the window pane, and after the light of the room, the garden appeared completely dark, and I could distinguish nothing at first. I was beginning to feel I had imagined the opening of the gate. Susy did bark occasionally at night, and there had never been anything to account for it before. Then, as I was about to turn away from the window, I saw a gleam of light moving away from the orchard. It flickered around the goat pen and then the goat house, and there it stayed. I had a ridiculous feeling that someone wanted to steal the animals. The goats would certainly resist such a manoeuvre. I pictured the stubborn strength of King Billy when he was being led one way and wanted to go another, and remembered the racket the little one always made if anything unsuual happened. And then I thought of Darkie.

I put my coat on and made for the veranda door. While the intruder was up the garden I could quite easily slip across to the chalet and rouse Eric. But once outside it was not so easy. I hadn't dared take a light, and apart from the difficulty of the darkness my legs felt unsteady. Then I nearly fell over something sprawled on the lawn. I discovered it was a bicycle.

Before I could get any further the small beam of light came zig-zagging down the path. It would cut me off completely from the chalet. The only thing to do would be to shout. I don't know if I could have managed this or not, but before I could try a little voice piped, "Here's another shed!" and this remark was followed by a loud "Sh-h-h!"

Children! I groped back to the house and fetched the hurricane lamp. Outside the stable I confronted them, and asked, "What exactly are you supposed to be doing?" in what I hoped was a good imitation of a school-teacher's voice.

In the circle of yellow light stood a boy of about twelve, a dot of a child beside him. I recognised that solemn little face and those knowledgeable eyes. This was Gerry of the woods, who had been looking for "the donkey lady" and had wanted to see Darkie kneeling in her stable on Christmas Eve. So he had made it—even without an invitation.

"This is Gerry," said the big boy hurriedly. "You told him in the woods he could come and see the donkey on Christmas Eve."

I hoped my expression was sufficiently stern.

"That's the first I've heard of it," I said. "I remember Gerry and talking about the donkey, but I didn't say he could come here at this time of night. Did I, Gerry?" I added severely.

"You said you'd talk about it if you saw me again," he informed me with devastating accuracy. "So I come."

The logic of this seemed perfectly clear to Gerry if not to me.

"To see me?" I countered. "You didn't, you know. You came to see the donkey. Without permission." I turned to the other boy. "Does your mother know?"

He shook his head.

"This isn't the way to do things," I told them severely. "You came out when you should have been in bed, and you've been creeping about this garden where you've no right to be frightening the life out of me. I think you'd better both go straight home. Are you going to get back all right?"

"Oh, yes," he said. "I brought him on my bike. He's

my brother. It doesn't take long." He looked at me earnestly. "I only wanted him to see the donkey. We didn't mean no harm. Honest, we'd have knocked at the door, only we thought you'd be asleep. I know you'd have let him look if we'd knocked."

This was perfectly true. He knew it and I knew it, but I said, still stern, "Your mother will be worried."

"She won't," he assured me. "She won't know."

But it was Christmas Eve. I suddenly thought of their mother, or father, or both, going quietly into their bedroom to fill stockings and then finding it empty.

"Of course she will!" I exclaimed. I looked at the little boy. "Gerry, don't you think Father Christmas will tell her? When he goes into your bedroom and finds your bed empty? Then what will she do?"

"We saw Father Christmas in the shop," said Gerry. "He's not comin' to our house tonight."

"I left a note for mum," said the big boy hurriedly. "You know, just in case she looks in. But she won't. I know she won't." He put a hand on my arm, and his eyes were appealing. "If you let him look at the donkey I'll come up tomorrow and Boxing Day and muck out the stable for you."

"I'll muck out the stable too!" said Gerry.

I laughed. "Look, I'm not going to make a deal of it. Of course you can see the donkey now you're here, but—"

Gerry nearly let out a whoop.

153

"You'll have to be very quiet," I said, "or you'll disturb her. Come on—this way."

And then I hesitated. They were going to be disappointed if they saw Darkie merely standing or, worse still, pushing her nose out for tit-bits when she should have been taking part in the adoration of the beasts.

"Of course," I said, "it isn't midnight yet, you know. Not," I added hastily, "that you can wait till then. And in any case Darkie might not like being interrupted."

"We won't make a sound," the older boy whispered.

I felt their keen excitement as I looked at their bright faces. There seemed to be nothing I could do, beyond find soothing words to account for Darkie's unChristmas-like behaviour when I opened the door. I suddenly thought of all the people for whom Christmas is a time of sorrow, when grief, pain or disillusionment take the place of joy. And now these children on a quest of happiness and satisfied desire . . . no Father Christmas calling at their house, and a perfectly ordinary donkey with inquisitive nose in a stable instead of a reverent donkey at prayer. Those who lost the joy of Christmas might derive comfort from unexpectedly finding that there is a state of peace in which one may live in protection from the hurts of life, but what did these children know of that? They would have to live through many experiences before they made this discovery.

I could have prayed Darkie would be kneeling but how to pray for the seemingly impossible? Yet words

were in my head . . . "Ask and receive . . ." "All things
are possible . . ."

Surely the only stipulation was that one must *believe*.

At that moment the extent of my belief was that I could,
in some way, ease the children's disappointment.

It was not until I had opened the top door of the
stable and held the lamp aloft that I remembered. I saw
little Gerry hoisted up by his brother and I heard
Gerry's awed whisper. "She's *kneeling* . . ."

How many times, when I had come to the stable late had I seen Darkie in just that position. Rising on her knees from her lying position to greet me. To the child in the soft yellow lamp-light, caught up in the enthralment of Christmas, in the magic of the story, it did indeed seem that he had actually witnessed her in the act of really kneeling. Kneeling to adore the Christ child on Christmas Eve. His own solemn little face looked angelic in that moment, and I felt an intense gratitude.

Darkie came forward and Gerry leaned over the door and kissed that broad forehead.

"There, Darkie!" I said. "You've never been kissed before, have you?"

The big boy was beaming.

"Darkie's a *good* donkey," said the little boy.

We were speaking in whispers, standing there almost in awe within the halo of lamplight. Wonderment was in the child's face, joy on the face of his brother, and the donkey for once stood motionless, not seeking anything with her nose. As for me, I felt light and uplifted with happiness.

Really there was no more to be said. They stole away from the stable hand in hand, collected their bicycle and went off quietly. No chattering, not even "Good-bye." One doesn't say ordinary things at a magic moment.

When they had gone Darkie slowly rubbed her chin on the stable door with her long, slow, satisfying movement. Now her nose sought my hand. Her eyes were deceptively innocent, but her nose was saying, "Well, I did my bit, didn't I, and they've gone, so now I can be an ordinary donkey again and have something to eat. Can't I?"

"All right," I whispered. "You can!"

And I almost ran to fetch the biscuit tin before she opened her mouth and bawled irreverently into the night.

A ND so we come to the end of our year, Darkie's and mine. Winter arrives in earnest, and the cart is put away, my travels in it over for the time being.

This year, sitting in retrospect by a log fire sparking merrily up the chimney, I thought of all those travels from its very beginning—that first trip to the woods, on my birthday in January. Would we make it again next year, Darkie and I? Both of us still sturdy and willing, all that was needed were a few hours of fair weather.

I had travelled out to meet the spring, and all along the way I had seen almost every individual leaf uncurl from pin-point to crinkle of green into its own identity, and down every hedgerow and among the trees in the wood I had witnessed the subtle change from the first faint green mist to the greenest of all greens, which is spring at its height, and then to the gradual darkening and deepening during summer growth and weather contact to the varnished colours of autumn.

I had seen processions of flowers, the daily routine of birds, fields joyous with lambs, and the pomp and panorama of the ever changing skies. People too—as many as if I had walked a London street. All were friendly, and the smiling and waving had made me feel like a queen in my cart.

And I had dreamed along the solitary lanes, my heart and mind filled with activity as my body sat motionless, the reins slack in my hands, my dreaming donkey nodding to a standstill.

I had enjoyed it all—field and wood and sea, the great openness and the deeply sheltered places, the sun and wind on my face and morning air straight off the hills and the sea.

Yes, it had been a good year.

I went to the window, and there was Darkie's white powder puff of a nose stuck out over her door again as she waited for someone to notice her. She had seen me . . . up went her head and out came that vigorous voice.

I answered obediently. Listening to her tranquil crunching of carrots, I found myself thinking how fortunate I was not to be imprisoned in a room. In different circumstances I might well have been. I thought of the many people of my age who were struggling for their very existence in their one lonely room, or bravely adapting, or failing to adapt, perhaps, to life in strange new surroundings, away from the familiarity of home. Maybe they would not have wanted a donkey and cart, as I had, but they would want the blessings of contentment and peace, comfort and interest and the spice of variety in their daily lives. They would need to escape mentally and spiritually from life's hardness and restrictions, from grief and loneliness.

It had taken a donkey to liberate me—and not simply from being housebound. Stroking her nose, I reflected that even if I no longer drove out in the donkey cart I now had a whole inner world to illumine the outer, in whatever circumstances I might happen to be. In my intense gratitude I could only wish that everyone who was mentally as well as physically enclosed, as I had been, might find the freedom of the universe. To find it mentally is to have the greater treasure.

There were no more carrots. Contented, my satisfied donkey slowly rubbed her chin on the lower half of the stable door as I confided my thoughts to her.

"Well, Darkie," I said, "you're in better shape than Modestine after your journeys. But then *you* didn't have to walk a hundred and twenty miles in twelve days."

She looked at me with calm dark eyes. There was understanding between us, and she had no complaints. Like Stevenson and his donkey we had been fast companions.

Soon, I promised myself, I would start another year of travels in a donkey trap.